T0356641

MISSION:
Invincible Marriage

MISSION: Invincible Marriage

A Battle-Tested Guide to an Enduring Relationship

JASON & ERICA REDMAN

wm

WILLIAM MORROW

An Imprint of HarperCollins*Publishers*

This book is dedicated to our children, Phoenix, Angelica, and Mackenzie, or as we know them, Austin, Sierra, and Aspen.

It has always been our goal as parents, and husband and wife, to show you through example what a healthy, strong, invincible team should look like.

We pray that all three of you will find your most important teammate and build your own Invincible Marriages.

This book is also dedicated to all the Protector couples who have struggled through the hardships of balancing the mission and adversity of protecting, in law enforcement, fire services, and military service, with the struggle of marriage and raising children in this dangerous and often chaotic environment. We salute all of you who have endured with your own invincible marriages but also provide this book as a guide to help others achieve their own invincible marriages and lives of happiness and success.

CONTENTS

FOREWORD BY GARY SINISE

How does a marriage survive when everything around you feels bleak? When it's hard to hope? Like most marriages, those days can be challenging. For my wife and I, we rely on our faith, our sense of humor (very important), and we look for examples—people who have somehow made it through the dark to the other side. Time and time again, the resilience and perseverance of our heroes has been a light for me.

For nearly forty years, I've had the honor of supporting our veterans, military, and first responder communities. I've had a front-row seat to hear their stories: people who get knocked down by deployments, injuries, crisis, and loss. Our heroes just keep getting up and showing up, knowing full well it may cost them their lives. They refuse to quit. They refuse to let it defeat them. And in some cases, that singular focus that makes them incredible heroes comes at the expense of their relationships.

I saw it acutely when I had the honor of playing combat-wounded Lieutenant Dan Taylor in the film *Forrest Gump*. Lt. Dan had a single-minded commitment to service, so he lost more than his legs when he was injured. He lost his sense of identity and purpose. That kind of sacrifice impacts not just the warrior, but everyone around them. And even for those who aren't injured physically, the job, with all its risks and unpredictability, can test even the strongest bonds.

Marriage is often a casualty of service. The divorce rate in our protector communities is significantly higher than for the rest of us. We all face adversity, but the unique nature of their work puts pressure on their relationships daily. It's difficult to watch someone you love face risk, face death day after day. There's a battle fatigue that sets in, no matter how much you love each other.

I've been married nearly fifty years, and we've had some very tough days.

When facing adversity in a marriage, examples of relationships that have faced that darkness together and won can inspire us and help to lead us out of the darkness. Couples whose resilience and commitment to each other made their marriage a training ground that only strengthened them when the unimaginable struck.

When I think of a marriage facing great challenges, two people persevering, overcoming, and thriving, I think of my friends Jason and Erica Redman. I first met the Redmans when Jay was recovering from numerous combat injuries after his SEAL unit had been ambushed in Iraq in 2007. When I saw them look at each other, I could tell Jay and Erica were one of those couples who not only persevered through one of the most difficult situations a relationship can face, but they thrived. Here was a guy who had taken machine-gun fire to his face and body, lived through it, and fought back to finish his military career. Erica and their kids stood beside him every step of the way. That kind of life-altering injury has ended more marriages than we can count. But Jay and Erica treated it like a training ground instead of a graveyard for their marriage. They leaned into their partnership and deepened their commitment.

Even under the best conditions, marriage is hard because life is hard. And whether you're in the protector community or not, a strong marriage doesn't just happen. Just like becoming a SEAL or firefighter or EMT, it requires training, testing, and perseverance. It requires patience, focus, and attention. It takes coordinated effort. Jay and Erica applied that mission mindset to their marriage, and they invest and protect each other with a ferocity that's inspiring.

Life can certainly twist and turn and sometimes it can take a brutal toll on your marriage. The question is will you let it defeat you, or will you work together to create something invincible?

MISSION:
Invincible Marriage

INTRODUCTION

I Survived an Ambush but Almost Killed My Marriage

One morning, four years after I'd been shot in the face in Iraq, my wife Erica and I drove out to Suffolk, Virginia, to scout a location for one of our nonprofit's skydiving events. I don't remember if the radio was on or off, if it was sunny or overcast. But as we sat there in the truck, miles apart in our minds, Erica began a conversation that would scare me shitless.

"Hey, Jay," she said softly, "this is how it starts." It wasn't an accusation. It wasn't a judgment. It was an observation.

I tightened my grip on the steering wheel. "What is?"

"Months or years from now, if we don't fix this, we're going to look back and say this is where it started. The beginning of the end of this marriage. This quiet. Trying to deal with stuff alone and shutting each other out. I don't want that. We have to do something different. We fix things together, remember?"

I nodded, keeping my eyes on the road, perspiration beading my forehead, my body tense with the truth of what she was saying. After a decade of marriage, divorce had never been an option for us, but her words hit me in the gut. I felt the defensiveness rise in my chest. I wasn't sure I *could* fix this.

SOME MARRIAGES END with a flash of conflict that finally explodes into separation. Other marriages end the moment an infidelity begins. I put my marriage at risk not in the chaos of conflict or indiscretion and not even in combat, but in a cold quiet that shut my wife out. In my mind I had good intentions: I was dealing with my own darkness, fighting a hungry dragon that I had brought home from the battlefield and had taken residence in my mind. I didn't want her to have to manage it. But those warped intentions could have obliterated the strongest, most valuable asset in my life: my marriage.

How could I survive an entire SEAL career, life-threatening combat injuries, forty surgeries, and now screw up this one relationship that had supported me unconditionally? It's easier than you think.

In 2013, life should have been great. It *was* great. I had survived getting shot in the face and body in a combat ambush, I was past most of my surgeries, I had climbed Mount Rainier and discovered I could still ski with my family. My retirement from the Navy was on track, I'd written and sold a book that was about to come out, and our nonprofit seemed to be doubling in size every year. I had it all. My wife Erica, whom I called my long-haired admiral, had stuck with me through every obstacle. I had a beautiful wife, healthy kids, and a stable future steeped in purpose.

But the process of retirement from the Navy was taking its toll, along with the aftereffects of my injuries and experiences. I was having trouble sleeping, and in the final months of my Navy career, I had abandoned the physical discipline of working out and eating well because I was so busy trying to keep the nonprofit going while I was coming to grips with leaving a job I loved. I was in my head and overwhelmed. I felt numb. I'd work all day at my office on base, come home and work on the nonprofit, and then retreat to our bedroom and shut the door, thinking if I could just be alone long enough to get some quiet, I could get my mind right. If I could just get a good night's rest, I could face my wife and kids to be who they needed. Just one more scotch and more time.

Erica was kicking ass with the nonprofit, managing our household and kids, all the while trying to reconnect with me. She tried to get me to go out to dinner or watch a movie, even just sit together. Even when I went through the motions and joined her, I wasn't *with* her. And I could feel it—the distance opening up. I blamed myself. I needed to fix this funk I was in. Then I could reconnect with her.

This went on for weeks. I'd stopped going to the girls' dance studio and Austin's soccer games. I was so tired, and life was moving so fast as retirement and the book and nonprofit events barreled toward us in quick succession. I felt like I was flying an airplane that had every warning light and emergency alarm blaring in my mind. I couldn't figure out how to fix it, and there was no place to land. I thought if I could get everything to stop for a minute, I could deal with it. I was the "overcome" guy—the "never-quit" guy. I did NOT want to ask for help. I could do this myself.

But I wasn't paying attention. I didn't see the big picture. Or if I did, I didn't want to face it. That morning, Erica and I drove out to Suffolk, as panic squeezed my chest and two moments replayed in my mind: the day I should have died and the day Erica walked into the hospital confident we would get through my life-altering injuries together.

In 2007, I was caught in a deadly ambush with my SEAL team in Iraq. I took machine-gun fire across my body and face and lay on the desert floor while my team finished the firefight. In that moment, I knew I was bleeding out—death was imminent unless my team could clear the field and get me back to the hospital. All I wanted was one more day with my wife and kids, one more birthday, one more Christmas. I chanted to myself, "Stay awake to stay alive." I knew that if I was still conscious by the time I got to the hospital, I would have a far greater chance of getting back home alive.

I did make it to the hospital, and within days I was back stateside to begin the long road to recovery. As I lay in that hospital bed in Bethesda, half my head wrapped, my body broken, tubes and wires and IV lines running everywhere, I was terrified. Erica would soon see me for the first time. I knew guys whose wives had walked away in the face of combat injuries. It was too much, especially if they hadn't had a strong marriage to begin with. I didn't even want to look at myself in the mirror. I felt like a horrific monster. Would my beautiful wife be repulsed by how I looked? Would the docs be able to put me back together? What kind of life would we have even if they could? Questions pulsed through me. I wanted to see her more than anything, but I didn't want her to see me. Not in this weakened, broken state. Maybe if I had more time to heal, it would be easier to see her. But she wouldn't be deterred.

Erica walked through that hospital door, her long blond hair fluttering behind her, her signature sweet but strong smile spreading across her face. God, she was a vision. She didn't recoil, take a single step back, or even flinch. She marched up to my bed, gingerly kissed me through the tubes and wires, and gripped my good hand.

"We're going to get through this—together," she said. Her resolve shone through her eyes. My relief was palpable. I had married an angel. And she was going to stay no matter what it took. Staying awake had kept me alive in Iraq, and I was never more grateful to be alive than in that moment.

As I recovered in that hospital bed, other visitors came and went. I couldn't speak due to the extent of my facial injuries. One group in particular came in while I was dozing, but I distinctly heard them pitying me, like they'd written me off as someone forever damaged. I was enraged. When Erica came back to the room, I wrote out what had happened and told her, "Never again." I wrote out a note that I had Erica put on the door to advise visitors to check their pity at the door. It was written on regular white printer paper, and after another visitor came through with pity, clearly missing the sign, I told Erica I needed poster paper. She came back with an eleven-by-seventeen piece of neon orange paper, and in black Sharpie, I wrote out the sign that would go viral. I wrote:

ATTENTION TO ALL WHO ENTER HERE

If you are coming into this room with sorrow or to feel sorry for my wounds, go elsewhere. The wounds I received, I got in a job I love, doing it for people I love, supporting the freedom of a country I deeply love. I am incredibly tough and will make a full recovery. What is full? That is the absolute utmost physically my body has the ability to recover. Then I will push that about 20% farther through sheer mental tenacity. This room you are about to enter is a room of fun, optimism and intense rapid re-growth. If you are not prepared for that, go elsewhere.

From: The Management

Erica put it on the door. A fellow SEAL pinned his Trident to it. When it went viral online, not only did it inspire others to push through their recovery, but it brought my family to the Oval Office to meet with President Bush. Our advocacy for this community we love became public on a national stage.

I would apply my SEAL mindset to recovery and every aspect of my life, experiences outlined in my first book, the *New York Times* bestseller *The Trident,* and further explained in my second book, *Overcome.* Our resolve was tested so many times over the next few years, but through it all, Erica was there. She had hard days, too, but we acknowledged them together and kept pressing.

That's why when I sat in that truck headed to Suffolk, I felt my world closing in. She had seen me with my face half blown off, she'd been a full-time caretaker for me as I recovered, she'd held my hand, strong and steady. The thought that I might be able to push her away so far that I'd lose her, that I'd lose our life, scared the life out of me. I didn't want to live without her. But I also didn't want people to see my weakness. I was supposed to be the "sign on the door" guy—resilient, unwavering. How could I survive an ambush, all these surgeries, and nearly kill my marriage?

She sat beside me quiet, waiting. The road signs whizzed past in a blur. I was tired of the numbness, of going through the motions. She was right. This was more than a few bad days. This was a problem.

It was time to stay awake to stay alive again—wake up, and stay awake, to keep my marriage alive. A few minutes passed, and while I was still defensive inside, still exhausted, still irritated that we'd even had to have this conversation, I made a choice.

"Okay. I'll go talk to someone."

The tension in the cab diminished. When Erica silently reached her hand across the seat, I took it. She didn't ask a lot of questions. She didn't demand answers on a timeline. She didn't issue ultimatums. She trusted me to take action, and her hand in mine, like that day in Bethesda, meant she was still here for the long haul. I didn't know what I was going to do yet. I didn't feel like letting anyone into the dark place that was my mind. I knew things weren't fixed yet. But I knew I was going to try. I didn't have any more time to waste. I didn't want to lose this woman who had walked through fire with me.

A key part of my success as a SEAL, as a man, was due to strong relationships, especially those with my wife and family. It even became one of the tenets I coined and live by: "Love greatly." At that time, I didn't have all the words to explain what made Erica and me a great team, but I knew that I was a better SEAL, a better business partner, and a better man with her by my side. Every time I speak at events, someone will ask me about Erica, about her journey, about how she's stayed strong, and sometimes about why she's stayed with me so long. As if I haven't asked myself the same damn thing. I am a lucky man. But strong marriages take more than luck.

In the last year of my Navy career, I worked on Admiral Bill McRaven's task force for the Preservation of Force and Family. We looked at data from several years of military service and found that the high tempo of war had taken a serious toll on Special Operation Forces and their families, a course McRaven intended to correct. The task force found that service members with strong family relationships were better operators, healthier long term, and more stable after they left military service. In short: the task force found that strong marriages and families are an asset. Despite the old saying that "If the Navy'd wanted you to have a wife, they'd have issued her with your sea bag," suddenly the research showed that it was worth the time and money to help sailors and other service members build and maintain strong family connections.

That investment was long overdue. Military life is hell on a marriage. The moves, the training, the deployments, the transition—all of it wears on relationships. In the special operations world, the toll is even greater. Our divorce rate is nearly 90 percent in the SEAL teams. The high tempo coupled with high risk and the demands of the job obliterate most marriages around us. As SEALs, we're highly trained to face every kind of obstacle that could possibly present itself on the battlefield. But at home, we're losing the war for our marriages. Why? I think it's three things: We don't treat marriage as a No Fail mission, where the consequences of failure have catastrophic impact, although our marriages *should* be like that. We don't train like our lives depend on it. We don't communicate like it matters. And ultimately, our spouses don't feel like our most important teammate. So, when your marriage comes under fire, you can't withstand the heat. We refuse to quit in almost every area of our lives. We should be uniquely qualified to get through tough times in a marriage, yet we aren't. It doesn't have to be this way. If the military can recognize the investment needed in marriage, as couples, we can too. Whether you're married or single, military or civilian, you need a new perspective on marriage. Invincible marriages don't just happen. They are built from communication with a clear mission and intentional training. That's what we intend to show you in this book. How we faced those same odds of failure, and instead of folding, Erica and I emerged stronger than ever. You can too.

Men, many of us have made our marriages into an obstacle, instead of the asset they can be. What do you do with assets? You make it your mission to guard them, you tend to them, you defend them from attacks, and if you want them to grow, you sure as hell don't ignore them. It's time to wake up and take the action needed to protect the most precious relationships in our lives. We shouldn't have to be bleeding out in the desert to recognize that in the end, our family is all that will matter. It's time to protect your marriage as an asset. It's time to approach your marriage like a mission. That's what this book will help you do.

Before we begin, one caveat: If you're in an abusive situation where you or your children are being harmed, it's time to go. Don't think it can't happen to you. Domestic violence touches every single socioeconomic, political, racial, and geographic demographic out there, and you cannot address it while you're still in the line of fire. Can your spouse change? Maybe. But you cannot continue to put yourself and your kids in danger while they work it out. There are a number of good resources at the National Domestic Violence Hotline. You can call 800-799-7233 or go to their website at https://www.thehotline.org.

ERICA AND I aren't professional therapists or marriage counselors. There are tons of great books out there by those professionals, and you should read them. We certainly have. Erica and I are real people who've walked through fire together and care about helping others navigate marriage with the overcome mindset that has carried us through the last twenty years. You might not be a military couple facing deployments or combat injuries, but if you're facing adversity that makes your marriage feel like a battlefield instead of a refuge, this book is for you. If you're single or dating and eager to make sure you go into marriage with your eyes wide open, with tools to make your partnerships indestructible, this book is for you too. And to our protector community—veteran, military, first responders, law enforcement—we see you. We know how much you sacrifice. Don't let your marriage be collateral damage in that fight. Use this book to build an indestructible marriage that supports you through your challenging and necessary work.

I think it's important to say that you might need more than this book to transform your marriage. You may need professional help like I did. After that day in the truck, I went to see the chaplain and psychologists in our unit and began a conversation. When I found a treatment program that addressed the physical and mental issues that troubled me, I signed up and followed through, and for me, that professional help drastically improved my sleep and mental function. I let go of my pride and took action because I recognized that while my mindset was critically important, sometimes the body needs help processing. Sometimes professional therapy is necessary. Getting help is not a sign of weakness. It's one of the most courageous things you can do. And as you address those physical, mental, and emotional needs, you are showing your spouse that you care enough about your marriage to do what needs to be done.

That's the invincible marriage mindset we unpack in this book, and don't worry! I (Jason) only wrote the intro from my point of view. The rest of the book you'll hear from both of us.

How to Use This Book

Our hope is that you use this book to clarify your marriage's mission and learn how to be unwavering teammates for each other, the same way SEAL training builds courageous and highly skilled teams who protect each other as they complete complicated and dangerous missions. For some of you, that means right now while you're dating, you learn to communicate, to share your values and priorities, and to become the best partner possible—the earlier you start training, the more prepared you'll be. For some of you, you're already married and looking for resources to strengthen your partnership. Dive in—start training. For some of you, you're in crisis. This book is a triage station that can help you begin to heal, one decision at a time, as you choose to protect and defend your marriage.

PART I: MISSION

This section helps you define your mission and opens up channels of communication. We begin with friendship. **Chapter 1: Commit to Friendship** outlines three steps to restore the friendship that needs to be the foundation of your marriage.

Chapter 2: Build Your Invincible Values will challenge you to reexamine your beliefs and to make sure you align on the things that matter most.

Once you have identified your core values, **Chapter 3: Set Clear Priorities** asks you to look at how you spend your time, energy, and resources in your marriage.

PART II: TRAINING

Part II gives you practical steps to begin your training together in marriage. From rituals to communication, you have to practice if you want an invincible marriage.

Chapter 4: Establish Rituals speaks to the surprising power of creating rituals in your marriage to strengthen your intimacy and trust.

If you've ever asked yourself, "Is this it?," then check out **Chapter 5: Support Each Other's Dreams**. Ignoring your dreams may be causing friction in your marriage, and we'll show you how to start dreaming together again.

Chapter 6: Adjust Your Mindset is about so much more than positive thinking. It's about how complacency and control can undermine your marriage unless you actively counter it.

And while every chapter will build your communication skills, we had to include a full chapter on it, and **Chapter 7: Improve Communication** delivers the techniques we use to keep the channels between us open.

PART III: UNDER FIRE

This section focuses on how to handle the toughest moments of marriage. Here's where your shared mission and training begin to pay off.

Chapter 8: Face Conflict Together reframes the way you see conflict in your marriage to make sure you're fighting on the same side, *for* each other.

Through the various challenges and seasons of marriage, there are times you need space. **Chapter 9: Know When to Give Space** gives practical tips for what to do when you're overwhelmed and how to keep coming back together. Don't miss the story about how I broke up with Erica while we were dating, and she used space *very* effectively.

Chapter 10: Turn to Humor can help you take yourself less seriously while building a stronger relationship, essential in the middle of a firestorm.

Chapter 11: Support in Failure is a master class on how Erica supported me through a couple of situations that might have ended my career. In this chapter, you'll learn how to be a safe harbor and support each other in tough times.

Finally, there are a couple of bonus chapters about topics that always come up when we talk to people about our marriage: kids and business. Check out how we keep our marriage strong as we raise kids and run businesses together in those sections.

IN EACH CHAPTER, we'll share stories from our life and from others like us who have been in challenging careers like the military, law enforcement, and first responder communities. You'll learn about the principles that have made our marriage strong, as well as how to commit and build habits that will make your marriage the asset you want it to be. And because we know ideas are worthless without action, each chapter has a section at the end with an Invincible Marriage Moment to help you take your first steps toward change. Those investments in your most important teammate can carry you through even the worst crisis you can imagine. And if you're sitting there thinking, "We're not really in a crisis, Jason, maybe we can skip some of this," let me tell you this from experience: Crisis is coming. It's part of life. Don't wait until everything's off the rails to invest in your marriage—that's the moment when this work pays off. That day in our truck, Erica had spent over a decade loving me, supporting me in success and failure, sharing values and priorities, creating conditions in our marriage where she knew how to best communicate that we were in trouble in a way I could hear her.

And I did.

I listened and took action because for over a decade, I'd been investing in Erica, too—listening to her, learning when she needed space, sharing her dreams, becoming best friends. We'd created a battle-worthy invincible marriage that was still an asset, and I wasn't about to let that ship go down without a fight. Like Erica said, "We fix things together." She was right. You can fix things together too.

Regardless of where your relationship is today, Erica and I know that it's not too late to take an honest look at yourself and your marriage. Is it an asset or an obstacle? If it is an asset, I hope this book helps you invest in, protect, and grow that asset. If it's an obstacle, it's time to face it and change it. That is the Overcome Mindset I speak on all across the country. A mindset that says for every obstacle there is an opportunity. Your marriage is no different. You went into your marriage because you believed in it. It's time to fulfill that original belief.

Will it be easy? No, but nothing worth having comes easy. Consistent effort yields results. You don't need a grand gesture or a miracle. Stop waiting around wasting time and start moving the needle on the greatest relationship in your life. It's worth the battle to treat your marriage like the high-level mission it is. It's time to get after it.

PART I

MISSION

Are you treating your marriage like a mission? If you want an invincible marriage, you first need to commit to your most important teammate and clarify your shared mission. That mission is grounded in friendship and fueled by shared values and priorities.

CHAPTER 1

Commit to Friendship

O ur relationship started with a lie.

It was a mostly harmless lie of necessity, but it eventually became an obstacle we had to face to take our relationship seriously. To begin real friendship and commitment.

We met at a club in Louisville, Kentucky. Jason was twenty-four. He was out with his SEAL teammates, who needed a cover story to avoid drawing attention to their elite SEAL status, which often led to stupid questions, drunken challenges, and sometimes even fights. That night, the cover story was that they were a team of boxers. Erica, twenty-two, was out with some girlfriends, ready to enjoy a night of music and dancing. It was just supposed to be a good time. A way to blow off steam after a busy week.

But then Jason saw Erica come through the door. There was just something about her. She seemed to glow, her sun-kissed skin against white pants and her crop top. When she smiled, Jason couldn't take his eyes off her. He offered to buy her a drink, and after a few minutes, she went to meet friends in another part of the club. Before the night was through, he'd tracked her down and initiated a conversation.

"Are you single? Why are you still single?" he asked.

Erica's answer would set the tone for the rest of the courtship: "I know what I'm looking for, and I haven't found it yet."

Erica had come out of a couple of unhealthy relationships,

one of them full of manipulation and drama. Between that reality and a family history of divorce and friction, she knew she was looking for someone who would meet her as an equal, and since she had an infant son, she needed someone who wanted a family. Someone who appreciated her independence and love of spontaneity.

Jason understood. He'd also experienced divorce in his family, and plenty of dating drama. He hadn't yet found someone who sparked the commitment needed for a long-term relationship.

Over a six-week period, we shared our histories and hopes, dreams and failures. All the while, Jason held on to that one lie that might have been a complete deal-breaker, afraid it might scare Erica away. You see, in a world of lies and deceit, most people don't believe you when you tell them you are a Navy SEAL. At the time, media portrayals of SEALs were limited to giant, muscle-bound types, but the reality was and is that SEALs defy physical categories—no matter their size or stature. Jason had seen teammates admit they were a SEAL in public, only to be answered with a snort and "Yeah, and I'm Princess Di." Additionally, for operational security reasons, most SEAL teams decide on a cover story when on the road to avoid revealing their true purpose or identity. From colleagues on a business trip to sports teams to friends on a hunting expedition, many stories have obscured the Navy SEAL reality. On this particular trip, we had a platoon mate who looked amazingly like professional boxer Oscar De La Hoya, so we leaned into it and claimed to be an amateur boxing team training with the US Army boxing team in Fort Knox, Kentucky. For the first six weeks of our dating life, Erica believed Jason was a boxer. Even when he met her family, Erica introduced him as a boxer, and Jason inwardly cringed when Erica's grandma, known as G.G., was impressed. Would she still be impressed when he revealed boxing was a lie? When he explained his real job? More importantly, would Erica understand? He'd never cared in the past—it was part of the collateral damage of being a Navy SEAL. But this time was different.

Jason's training in Kentucky was coming to an end, and he had a decision to make. This amazing woman had quickly become someone who consumed his thoughts, whose opinion mattered. There was no way he was heading back to Virginia without telling her the truth and hoping she'd stay with him anyway.

Let's Be Friends . . . Forever

The phrase "Let's just be friends" is a death knell for most romantic relationships, but ironically, marriages *not* founded on friendship fail. Why? Genuine friendship outlasts every season and every crisis when it is grounded in mutual trust. That's why choosing friendship is the first step into an indestructible marriage. You show your commitment on the daily through friendship.

Maybe you've seen those couples who radiate friendship even after years together, and you thought they were just lucky, an anomaly. But what if those couples who go the distance, who enjoy time together after years and crises, are actually doing something that you could easily emulate in your own marriage?

It all comes down to one belief. A study led by Samantha Joel of the Relationships Decision Lab at Western University found that the most powerful couple-variables that contributed to relationship satisfaction were not personality traits or compatibility, but beliefs, choices, and skills. The study of more than eleven thousand couples found that couples who *believed* their partner was committed and satisfied with the relationship reported far higher satisfaction. Just the belief! Can you imagine the impact you can make in your relationship just by changing your beliefs? This is why the first step of an invincible marriage needs to be an ironclad commitment to the partnership. It starts with beliefs.

We know firsthand about the power of belief because it was Jason's Overcome Mindset that carried him through SEAL training, leadership crises, and eventually combat injury recovery. That no-quit mindset and belief that we can overcome anything together still guides our marriage and business. But where did it begin? How do you know if you can trust someone enough to be vulnerable and show them your whole self? When we met, that was the question Jay kept asking himself as he debated whether or not to tell Erica the truth about his job and life. Would she stay? And if she did, was he ready to step into more commitment with her? In those early weeks of dating, we'd begun a friendship that neither of us had experienced before. That friendship is ultimately what made Jay take the risk to put it all on the line, and friendship is what helped Erica accept that challenge.

Think about your closest friendships. What are they like? Friendships forged in SEAL teams tend to last a lifetime. Why? When you willingly put your life into another man's hands and would die to protect him as well, it tends to create relationships that last. A couple of Jay's SEAL friends know everything about him: his secrets, his darkest fears, his doubts and insecurities. But friends also share in the moments of greatest joy and accomplishment. We have fun together. We find ways to hang out as often as possible. It doesn't mean we agree on everything. We don't. But those friendships stand the test of time because you've learned to depend on each other. You know if you call, they'll pick up. You enjoy time together. When you make mistakes, they aren't going to beat you down with it—they're going to commiserate with you, even if you both know that you're going to have to fix things later. You might not think about your friendships in terms of commitment, but isn't commitment just a kind of bond created by loyalty? We do things *for* each other and we do things *with* each other. That's why an invincible marriage begins with friendship, friendship founded in the belief that you're going to show up for each other time and time again. Friendship that says, out loud, "We're in this together. For life." Followed by actions that reinforce that belief and build your friendship day in and day out.

When life gets tough as a couple, you don't turn away from each other. When conflict sparks between you, you don't look for reasons to leave. When you feel disconnected, you don't hide out at work or consistently head to the bar with other people. You commit and follow through with the discipline needed to keep the promises you made. Early on, we decided that divorce wasn't an option. It wasn't something we pulled out in the middle of a fight and waved around as an ultimatum. When divorce isn't an option, when quitting isn't an option, you fight differently, and you approach tough seasons together with a shared focus. Commitment means you start thinking about your relationship over your own selfish wants and desires. You look out for the best interests of your partner, knowing that protecting them and investing in their success ultimately makes you both stronger. When you do that, both of you will believe you're in it for the long haul, and you'll spend less time looking over your shoulder wondering if it's going to last and more time actually enjoying each other. When you think about your closest friends right now, does that short list include your spouse? If so, great—use the rest of this chapter to press further into friendship. If your partner is not on that short list of your closest friends, it's time to restore your friendship, not just so your marriage will last, but so you both enjoy each other more along the way.

Three Steps to Restore Friendship

Once you've made that mental and verbal commitment, it's time to choose friendship. To restore your friendship, begin with vulnerability, time, and commitment.

Vulnerability

If you've had trouble connecting as friends in your marriage, or maybe you've had trouble making friends at all, let's look at how to take those first steps to friendship. How do you move into a stronger friendship?

Vulnerability.

For some of us, being vulnerable feels like a nonstarter. We are naturally protective of ourselves and our people. Maybe it's because vulnerability can feel like weakness when it lets others get close to us. To know us fully. Vulnerability is honesty. It means showing your partner everything, letting yourself be seen and in turn, seeing them fully. If you think about your closest friends, they are the ones who know the most about you, who see your faults and flaws, and like you anyway. Spend time with you anyway. Root for you anyway. How vulnerable do you allow yourself to be with your spouse? You don't have to go into a combat zone or intensive training together like SEALs do to open yourself to more vulnerability.

Another way to ask this question is to think about what parts of yourselves you try to hide. We're not talking about infidelity or destructive behavior here, just the everyday quirks and flaws that you tend to downplay while you're dating. Maybe you aren't even honest with yourself about those qualities. For example, when we were dating, we tried to keep our competitive natures in check when we played games (it didn't always work!). Maybe you're hiding some of your spending habits or a significant event from your past that affects how you show up in relationships. If you're going to deepen your friendship with your spouse, you're going to have to risk more vulnerability, and that starts with knowing yourself better. Can you start to notice the situations or triggers that make you happy, sad, or angry? What's under those reactions? Can you express them to your spouse or do you tend to minimize them to avoid being judged or hurt? If you grew up in a household where people didn't express emotions, this might be really uncomfortable. We're not saying you need to be overly emotional about everything all the time, but emotions are information, and that information can tell you a lot about how vulnerable you are in your relationships. For example, Jason is unflinchingly direct, which is often an advantage, but at times it can veer into insensitivity to Erica's feelings. She doesn't bottle those hurt feelings. She risks being vulnerable enough to call Jay on his insensitivity or to at least share how it made her feel. Instead of becoming defensive, both of us are honest about the interaction, apologize where needed, and emerge stronger.

Vulnerability requires us to be able to communicate what we need or expect. If you're someone who has always gotten along in the world by shape-shifting and trying to take on every other person's expectations, you might not even be sure of what you want. Can you tell your spouse that? You may need to spend some time thinking about what you want from your life and marriage, and then begin to explore that with your partner. Sometimes it's easier to begin by expressing what you know you *don't* want. We were clear from the beginning about what we didn't want. Hell, the first time Jason talked to Erica she told him she was single because she hadn't found what she was looking for, and she knew it wasn't drama or someone who couldn't commit to a family. Start rooting out the things you know you don't want and see what's left.

It's easy to skip this step. To play along, to make nice, to go through the motions and keep things peaceful on the surface. Over time, this will empty your relationship of any passion. You'll get five, ten, fifteen years down the road and wonder why you feel so lonely, even inside a marriage. Hiding can't sustain a relationship because it cuts you off from the very connection and intimacy that makes marriage so rewarding. Does it mean being open to being hurt? Yes. But that risk is why the reward is also so high. Stop putting on your battle armor inside your relationship and find ways to open up.

Vulnerability is an investment that pays off exponentially because that honesty is how you practice and strengthen trust. And trust is what will deepen your friendship and marriage.

Choose Time Together

It takes time and attention to build a high level of trust in any team. Those accumulated minutes, hours, and days will tell you if you click with someone, if you share interests and values. But you can't quit feeding that relationship once you're married. It surprises some couples to find out that they need to continue to make time for friendship to keep growing once they are married. Just like anything else in your life, if you ignore or starve something, it will die.

Time is the one resource you can't create, you can't purchase, you can't replace, and that is why when you choose to spend quality time together, it is an act that communicates commitment.

What if you are in a season of life where time is at a premium? Maybe you are building a business, or your kids are little and have more needs than you can keep up with. Maybe you are caring for a sick family member or just caught in a cycle where you feel more like roommates than partners. We get it. We've had those seasons, too, when prioritizing time together feels like too much effort, when it's just easier to stay late at work, when collapsing in bed is all you can manage. You can give in to those guilty habits that are weakening your marriage, or you can fight for your partner and a better life together.

"I'm able to be the best version of myself because of my wife," retired Navy SEAL Shane Kronstedt told us.

If you think you don't have enough time to pursue friendship with your spouse, let us tell you about Shane and his wife, Dr. Gabrielle Lyon, because they are *busy*. The Lyons have two crazy careers: She's the *New York Times* bestselling author of *Forever Strong* and a private practice physician. He's in a surgical residency. On top of that, they run a podcast, a small business, and have two small kids. We're sweating just thinking about all of that!

Here's the thing though: both Shane and Gabrielle are highly motivated, driven people, and when they talk about each other, you can hear the way their marriage and partnership is not just an enhancement, but actually the foundation of their success. Shane might work eighty to a hundred hours a week in his residency, and Gabrielle racks up extensive hours in her practice and business, but when they are home together, their time is focused. They commit to being present, making eye contact, and avoiding their phones and distractions. Even when they are exhausted, they make it a point to connect, have dinner as a family when possible, meditate together, and go to group workouts on the weekends when they can. Gabrielle said that anytime she notices they get short-tempered with each other, it's almost always because they haven't prioritized time together and they quickly *make* time for connection.

Look honestly at your calendar. How much uninterrupted time do you spend together now? If you have less than an hour a week, you are probably already in danger. If you're trying to maintain your physical fitness, you can be damn sure you're spending more than an hour a week to get strong. Why would building a marriage require less? If you are in a busy season, you might not have the ability to block off large chunks of time right now, but you can incrementally increase your time together each week or month. Set aside that time to be together. Make it sacred and don't use it for anything else.

Time is one way to tangibly communicate that you are committed to the marriage and to nurture your friendship. Let conversations go deeper. Linger and listen to each other. Take the time to show appreciation and let your spouse know that you are committed to them, because lip service can only take you so far. How else can you live out your commitment so that your partner sees it?

Commitment Out Loud

Jason loves to ski. It was one activity that Erica didn't share an affinity for. Scuba diving? Yes. Travel? Yes. Camping adventures? Yes. But not skiing. Erica had tried skiing once when she was sixteen. No lessons, improperly fitted gear, and inadequate winter clothing led to an absolutely miserable day and a decision to never do it again. In 2010, Jason wanted to take Erica and the kids skiing. Erica was not enthused—we had three small children and she had a household and business to run. Plus, the idea of revisiting that last failed skiing trip memory and spending a day freezing and falling on her butt sounded like torture. But she knew Jason loved skiing and wanted our kids to ski, so she agreed to go.

Skiing is not for everyone. There is no sport equivalent that prepares you for the mountain. Additionally, many people have a terrible first outing because they go with friends who are more proficient, and the novice ends up being left behind. The falling, the difficulty keeping your skis straight, and the embarrassment of trying to get up in the slippery snow all contribute to feelings of inadequacy. In short, it can expose a lot about a relationship.

Jason knew Erica would be focused on the safety and enjoyment of the kids over her own enjoyment and comfort. As with many other times in his life and military career, he knew that to make this work, he needed to find experts to help. On this trip, he had been invited by the Special Operations Command, Wounded Warrior Project, and the town of Whitefish, Montana, to bring our family out for not just skiing, but full-on lessons and personal instructors for every individual. After the requisite outfitting, practice at the base of the mountain, maneuvering and snowplowing, and several days of personalized instruction, the family came back together. It was finally time to tackle the ski lift and first hill together. We stood in line for the lift, Erica willing her skis to stay parallel, Jason corralling the kids forward. The snow-dusted Montana pines and crisp mountain air were a perfect backdrop, but Erica was just focused on slowing her breathing and getting through this first lift to the top of the mountain. The instructors settled the kids on their lift and Erica waved, praying someone at the top would help them if needed.

Now it was her turn.

She hadn't wanted to go skiing. Life already had shown her its fragility. Why barrel down an icy mountain on two slick pieces of wood? She looked over at Jason who was grinning at her.

"Ready?"

She didn't tell him she was worried she might faceplant and hold up the line. She didn't remind him that he still needed her to be the mother to our three kids. She didn't tell him her heart was about to beat out of her white ski jacket.

Instead, she nodded. She willed her legs to stay straight and wobbled as the lift came around. One of her skis slipped and panic gripped her, but Jason caught her arm to steady her as we were scooped up. Jason whooped and Erica exhaled as she fell onto the lift chair.

She'd done it!

Suddenly, all was quiet and she was able to see our surroundings. Erica looked at the colorful coats of skiers and snowboarders shooshing down various runs. It was so peaceful. She smiled and leaned into Jason. We were maybe halfway up the lift when we heard a woman in a purple jacket screaming at someone on the mountain. We could see her below and to the left, lying in the snow, one ski off, her other folded underneath her as she frantically pumped her arms all while continuing to yell at a snowboarder quickly approaching. He flew in so fast that he sprayed her with snow as he came to a stop and then reached out for her arm, a big grin on his face.

She slapped him away. Her voice carried all the way up the mountain. "Where were you? I've been here for fifteen minutes trying to get up!"

His shoulders sagged and he looked like he was responding.

"I can't believe you dragged me out here and left me! Worst day ever. I just want to go home!"

We couldn't hear his reply at first, but eventually his voice matched hers in volume.

"I THOUGHT you would figure it out! You wanted to go slow, so I said I would do a lap and come back. You said it was fine!" he shouted.

Erica resisted the urge to turn around to see what happened next. She could hear their voices trailing behind us.

"Happens all the time. I've seen so many couples blow up on a ski mountain," Jason said with a shrug.

As the combative couple was left behind, we continued up the mountain, enjoying the beautiful views.

The peace and quiet was short-lived. As we approached the top, Erica was terrified to get off and ski down the mountain. She turned her attention back to the task ahead. What had she been thinking when she'd agreed to this?

Erica looked over to the husband she had loved through so much. He was radiating with joy at having her on the slopes with him.

I can do this, she thought. The lift bounced, and she braced her skis to connect with the packed snow. With a jostle and bent knees, she scooted from the seat with relief.

We skied forward and linked up with the kids and the other instructors. "Let's go!" Jason said.

Erica took it slow. She expected to fall, but she knew she'd get back up. That's what she did. Always.

Jason stayed with her and the kids. Not lecturing, not coaching, just staying in step and encouraging her down the mountain. We laughed and shouted and admired the more adept skiers and hot-dogging snowboarders who passed. The three-year-olds ripping down the mountain with reckless abandon. Our own youngest daughter who only knew straight and fast but somehow could miraculously stop at the last second.

We were near the bottom, heading back to the lift, when Erica heard a familiar voice. It was the woman in the purple ski jacket, stomping off the mountain in her ski boots, unbalanced, with her skis and poles helter-skelter dragging behind her. The man was still reaching a hand out, offering to carry something, his snowboard under one arm. But she veered away from him, nearly toppling into the snow. Her words were hard to make out through the jagged sobs.

In the time it took the couple to march out of sight, we reached the lift. Erica felt the surge of relief and adrenaline at the same time. She'd done it!

"Want to take a break?" Jason asked.

The kids shouted to go again. Erica's feet were so cold and her legs ached. She looked to where the couple had disappeared.

"Let's go one more time. *Then* we can take a break," she said.

Jason leaned in to kiss her before snapping his goggles back on and turning toward the lift, Erica and the kids beside him.

IF YOU'VE EVER been skiing, you've witnessed a scene like that of the woman in the purple jacket. So many couples refuse to match pace—one person can't slow down enough to help his partner enjoy their time together. Or worse, you don't try new things together at all.

Jason stayed with Erica and chose not to get frustrated as Erica learned at her own pace. He recognized that skiing was new for her, and he adjusted his expectations. Instead of voicing that he was wasting time he could be spending on the slopes, he chose to appreciate the time with Erica. His love and friendship with Erica took priority over his own enjoyment of the activity. He knew he was investing in *her* enjoyment, and that might pay off later with a shared love of skiing.

This requires maturity and a level of emotional leadership many couples don't have. We've seen so many couples split while skiing, mostly due to unrealistic expectations. If you're hellbent on shredding down the mountain, don't expect to have an enjoyable fun-filled time of connection with your partner who is still learning. If you can't stay behind on the bunny hill without complaining or feeling put-out that you're having to wait, you're not choosing friendship. If you want your spouse to learn to do something you like, if you'd like to be able to share that activity, then you have to set aside your own proficiency and expectation of personal fulfillment to support your partner who's learning something new. That's what friends do.

Jason is still a stronger skier to this day, but he slows his pace to match Erica's often on the slopes because he genuinely enjoys the time with her and the kids. Although the kids can almost out-ski him now. Almost.

This is approaching marriage with a mission mindset. It doesn't mean doing everything together. It means when you are

together, you take the time to be on the same wavelength. To enjoy each other in the place where you each are, not the place you
wish you'd be.

HOW COMMITTED ARE you to friendship as the foundation to
your marriage? Are you only giving it lip service while you spend
too much time at work? Or maybe you haven't lived that commitment out loud for months or years and it's created a rift in your
relationship.

If you want to make your marriage an asset, if you want to
develop high-level trust, then it begins with rock-solid commitment that you don't just say out loud—you are living it out loud
every day. You are taking calculated risks to show your commitment.

When Jason realized he wanted more than another goodbye
that day in Kentucky, he knew the first step was to take the risk
of telling Erica the truth about his job and the toll it takes on
wives and families. He didn't sugarcoat it; in fact, he told her all
the reasons their relationship would likely fail. As a matter of
fact, after he finished telling Erica about his job as a SEAL, how
much he would likely be gone, and the 90 percent divorce rate, he
told her she should run. But his honesty and intensity convinced
Erica that it was worth the risk—that he would honor the commitment forged through friendship. Funny enough, that initial
deep, honest conversation has created a humor point throughout
the years. In hard times, when we're facing major adversity, one
of us will ask, "Is it too late to run?"

Then we both laugh and get back to attacking the problem.

The time we'd spent connecting translated to more than a short
fling. It was full of the attention and appreciation that makes
marriage last. No, not just last—become invincible.

INVINCIBLE MARRIAGE MOMENT

The first step to an invincible marriage is a mental and verbal affirmation of your beliefs: "We're in this together. For life." Then, you need to invest in your friendship again through vulnerability, time, and commitment out loud.

REFLECT

1. The research from the beginning of the chapter showed that marital satisfaction is highest when one simply believed their partner was committed and satisfied with the relationship. What do you believe about your partner right now?

2. How much time do you and your partner spend together each week? Be honest and talk about what each of you is choosing instead of time together.

3. Think about the couple who broke up on the ski slopes. What did each of them likely believe about the other that day? Why was it so destructive?

4. How is your friendship with your partner right now?

FIRST STEP

Make time to do something together in the next week or two that will rekindle your friendship. Find ways to encourage each other if it's uncomfortable, and express gratitude no matter how it goes.

CHAPTER 2

Build Your Invincible Values

By 2004, the Navy SEALs had a culture problem they couldn't ignore anymore. SEALs had always been expected to take risks, to operate under high-pressure situations, and to creatively attack problems, but those characteristics, without a guiding ethos, could also become dangerous qualities.

The precursor to the elite and mysterious SEAL teams began during World War II as specialized units, trained for underwater demolition. In May of 1943, the Chief of Naval Operations directed the Naval Demolition Project to meet "a present and urgent requirement." In June of 1943, the Naval Combat Demolition Unit training school was established in Fort Pierce, Florida, which became the foundation for SEAL Training as we know it today and the origin of the infamous "Hell Week" all SEAL candidates must endure. The Naval Combat Demolition Units (NCDUs) eventually swam into enemy territory on occupied beaches in Normandy and across the Pacific theater with explosives to clear the way for amphibious landings. NCDUs at Omaha Beach were awarded the Presidential Unit Citation; one of only three presented for military actions at Normandy, beginning a history of heroic action that would set the legacy of the SEAL teams for generations to come.

Those small teams continued to be developed and used through the Korean War and several smaller conflicts and crises, such as those in Laos and Cuba. By the time Vietnam was ramping up, Naval leaders recognized the rising need for a specialized force trained in unconventional warfare, with capabilities on land, air, and sea. In 1961, Admiral Beakley outlined the need to the Chief of Naval Operations, and by 1962, the first two formal SEAL teams were established, one in California and the other in Virginia. But even their existence was still highly classified and shrouded in mystery.

Part of the allure of SEALs even today is the unrelenting, scrappy, unconventional warrior ethos that has always marked our corps. In those early days after 9/11, special operation teams had to rework everything they'd learned about hierarchical military structure to better respond to an enemy that wasn't playing by traditional war rules. SEALs got good at making decisions on the fly, taking calculated risks, and learning communication protocols to debrief and do it all again. But the same characteristics that made men strong operatives also had the potential to destroy them from the inside.

In the early years of combat operations in Iraq and Afghanistan, SEALs and other Special Operation Forces were critically important, and we were being trained and prepared in grueling six-to-twelve-month training cycles, from the initial gauntlet of Basic Underwater and Demolition/SEAL (BUD/S) training to exercises and support in covert locations all over the world.

During one such exercise in Thailand in 2004, eight members of a SEAL platoon tested positive for cocaine. Two platoons were sent home and an investigation got underway. Coupled with other incidents involving sexual misconduct, domestic violence, drug and alcohol abuse, and other physical altercations, thirty-three SEALs were removed within a fifteen-month period—the largest loss of the SEAL teams to that date, even when you included combat-related deaths. It was a devastating blow.

In such a high-pressure environment where risk-taking was

valued and even expected, it wasn't unusual for SEALs to believe that any risk was worth it to accomplish the mission. It was easy to look at how we were kicking ass and ignore weaknesses or potentially morally gray areas in pursuit of our broader purpose. But that attitude had become a liability.

In 2005, a task force made up of fifty current and retired SEALs with a combined 745 years of operational experience completed an ethics assessment to identify the strengths and weaknesses of the SEAL teams to draft a set of values, an ethos, that would govern SEAL behavior on and off duty to restore trust in the elite forces and to ensure a warrior ethos was drilled into the next generation of sailors at every level.

Those guiding values strengthen the SEAL teams today, holding us accountable while at the same time inspiring us to lead ourselves and others to greatness.

Marriage, like our SEAL team missions, often begins with good intentions, but unless you are aligned in your values, those intentions can easily take you off course, create barriers between you, and damage the relationship from the inside. Why did you get married? What expectations did you bring with you?

Most people would say they got married for love and companionship. Some might say they wanted the formal commitment, either for religious or personal reasons. Others might say it made financial sense or because you both wanted kids. A 2019 Pew Research study confirms this, with 90 percent of married respondents saying they got married for love. But what is love? How does it change over time, or how does your understanding of it change over time? You intend to love each other. You expect to build a life together, but unless you know what is important to each of you, you may find you're not on the same page at all. Your marriage needs more than a vague declaration of love to guide you. You need a mission to love each other based on aligned values.

What Are Values?

Sometimes people think of values as solely an abstract idea, similar to the list of community principles that the SEAL ethos task force compiled in 2005, like courage, loyalty, and teamwork. And those qualities are values, but more importantly, a value is measured in behavior over time. Meaning, how those values show up in our everyday interactions will determine whether they build us up or destroy us.

When SEAL teams valued loyalty above all else, no one reported teammates or intervened when they were clearly breaking the law, endangering themselves and others with cocaine use. When courage and risk-taking isn't tempered by integrity and honor, those same values can be used to commit crimes as easily as they can be used to save vulnerable lives.

In marriage, values express what's most important to you individually and as a couple. Values are the beliefs that result in words and, most importantly, actions.

While dating, you can easily be swept away in the emotion and chemistry of a new relationship, and that excitement blinds you to the ways your beliefs might not align. When the novelty wears off, a year or two or ten down the road, so many couples stop and wonder what they ever saw in each other.

Special Forces marriages, along with those of law enforcement and first responders, are especially vulnerable to this clash of values, and maybe your marriage is vulnerable in the same way. The spec ops world has a nearly 90 percent divorce rate. For law enforcement and first responders, 60 to 70 percent will experience divorce over the course of their career. Why? We think it's a combination of things, but at the forefront are the challenges created by our high-tempo, demanding jobs—challenges that force us to make tough choices that reveal our values. The spec ops, law enforcement, and first responder world accelerates the process of finding out when your values as a couple don't align.

James Ward, OSS (Office of Strategic Services during World War II), outlined the conflict well in a short warning to younger operatives decades ago:

"Men, Special Forces is a mistress. Your wives will envy her because she will have your hearts. Your wives will be jealous of her because of the power to pull you away. This mistress will show you things never before seen and experience things never before felt. She will love you, but only a little, seducing you to want more, give more, die for her. She will take you away from the ones you love, and you will hate her for it, but leave her you never will, but if you must, you will miss her, for she has a part of you that will never be returned intact. And in the end, she will leave you for a younger man."

You might not be in Special Forces, but you probably have something that is constantly demanding your time, energy, and attention—something that is a source of conflict in your marriage, whether a job, children, habits, free time, and so on. It may be something you knew going in, like marrying a military service member, or it may be something that comes up as life progresses. Either way, the choices we make, through our behaviors, reveal our values. And when those values don't align or even attempt to meet each other in the middle, destruction is on the horizon.

We've watched marriage after marriage in our world crumble because when guys have to choose between their families or their career, they often choose the career. The job gives them a sense of purpose and meaning, confidence and predictability—traits not always easy to achieve in relationships, especially in those early years when you're still figuring it out. Their families *were* really important to them, and a big piece of why they were working so hard, but when something had to take a backseat, it was often their connection with their spouse.

When Jay was still on active duty, life was a revolving door of training and deployments. During any given month, he might be home for two weeks and out training for the other two weeks, while Erica worked and managed the household and kids. When appliances or cars broke down, she couldn't call Jay in from the field for help. Most people only think of military life as difficult during deployments. It *is* hard to have a service member away for extended periods of time. But what many don't grasp are the workups and travel required away from home even outside of deployments. How those weekly responsibilities back at home like taking out the trash, maintaining a home, or paying bills are in constant flux when a servicemember has an unpredictable schedule. When kids were sick or injured, Erica had to handle it. Even when his team was home in Virginia, Jay still had regular work responsibilities.

But as a couple, we had shared values about the importance of family. That meant when Jay's unit wasn't deployed or out of town training, he spent time at home with Erica and the kids. When he was gone, he made regular phone calls home, or as often as his remote locations allowed. Erica often heard from other spouses who were only getting sporadic calls from their husbands, and those couples essentially began living separate lives.

Values are behavior over time. Consider what your daily actions are communicating about your values, and get honest about the ways what you say doesn't align with what you do.

Initial Expectations

Just like the ethos and warrior mindset that is now standard instruction at basic training for the Navy, some values are important enough to understand from the beginning of a relationship.

But sometimes those deep conversations are ignored altogether due to immaturity or ignorance. Maybe you had those conversations, but the reality has changed or the words from those early days don't match up with today's actions.

When we first met, we quickly discovered that we shared several values and could work with each other on the rest. Both of us had come from homes of divorce, and we wanted partners who valued marriage as a lifelong endeavor and who wouldn't escalate into needless drama when problems came up. We both had a strong work ethic and weren't afraid to manage risk. Erica, once she knew Jay was a SEAL, agreed to support his career until his retirement, knowing it would likely be unpredictable and take its toll at times. Both of us wanted kids. Those were just a few of the core values that have carried us through twenty years of marriage. While we had an inkling early on that those shared values were important, we had no idea how they would shape the ways we responded to extreme adversity as a team.

So many special operation marriages begin with an illusion or a fantasy. There's an allure or mystique to marrying a Green Beret or a SEAL or a first responder, probably the same type of draw as professional athletes, celebrities, or power players in any field. Additionally, the way love is often portrayed in movies and culture, it's easy for any of us to enter a relationship with some sort of false expectations about the other person or marriage in general. Just like those SEALs ignoring the negative behavior of their teammates, dating couples sometimes overlook poor habits or behaviors and focus only on the positives.

Worse, you may notice a misalignment of values clearly from the outset, but believe you can change the person—or that marriage will change the person. We're not going to claim people don't change. They do and for a lot of reasons. But if you're going into marriage hoping to make someone into a person who is more compatible with your values? That's a recipe for disaster. The problem with misaligned values is that they are going to cause friction in a relationship—sooner or later.

If your wife wants kids and you don't, that is going to be a major source of resentment, possibly for years.

If one person has tight bonds with their extended family and they expect to spend holidays or vacations together while their partner doesn't want to spend time with extended family, every single holiday is going to be a battle zone.

If your spouse primarily values the security money offers through savings and investments while you love to spend on the regular, then that is going to create friction unless you negotiate some kind of compromise.

Whether it is family, money, faith, politics, how you spend your free time, or anything else that is important to you, returning to those core conversations can help you strengthen the foundation of your relationship, even if it is starting to crumble. Go back to the values and find ways to explain what is important to you and why—then respect each other enough to listen and compromise if needed to take care of each other.

Think back to those early days of dating and marriage. Be honest about what you said was important to you in a relationship. Does it line up with reality today? Why or why not? Can you list out the top three things that are causing friction in your marriage right now? What's at the heart of each of those arguments?

The early days of marriage can be a roller coaster. While it feels like the culmination of the dating period in your life, it's also a huge adjustment and a new beginning. Even if you were honest and open about the big things in life while dating—your work, family goals, finances, sex life, and faith—the day-to-day execution of those values will be a challenge to meld together. You might have a clear vision, even a mission for your marriage, but it will still require you to adapt. Part of what makes SEAL teams so effective is their ability to adapt on the fly, and they are able to do it because of the values they hold and the training they've completed. If SEALs are on a target and realize on arrival that the bad guys have moved next door, they are able to adapt the mission to move locations instead of calling the mission a failure and leaving the target area. You can do the same in your marriage.

On the night before our wedding, Erica had a stark introduction to the work hard, play hard culture of Jay's SEAL brotherhood that forced an adjustment even before we were wed. We'd planned a fun scavenger hunt with the guys versus the girls, but when Jay's SEAL buddies showed up, they had a much different agenda. They took him off alone, stripped him and tied him up, beat him with a swim fin, got him drunk, and then brought him back bruised and hobbling as a celebration of our marriage. That might sound harsh and ridiculous, but it was their way and Jay would have found it funny if his bride-to-be hadn't been so livid. We stayed up most of the night fighting and in tears, wondering if this marriage could go forward. Erica wasn't sure she could be a part of something she could not understand, especially on the eve of what should have been one of her happiest days. At the end of it, Erica realized that so much of the evening's shenanigans had been out of Jay's control. Yes, his SEAL buddies were wild and brutal in ways she didn't get, but they were also brave, loyal, and skilled. That night showed her that they had a bond that showed up no matter the circumstances and that while she might never fully understand his friends, she and Jason had more than enough overlapping values in every other area of life that she chose to trust him. To accept that his job and his teammates would be demanding, but that Jay would keep showing up for her and for them as a couple no matter what happened.

You might not experience that adjustment or doubt before the wedding, but it's coming. Here's an example we see all the time in the military: When you're dating someone in the military, you may or may not be aware of what the job requires—the amount of time it takes, the moves required, the training cycles. Most people expect deployments, and while those six to fourteen months apart are hard, there are so many other challenges, from the workups and training that require weeks away, to the moves that create grief and stress. Many couples find that they get married and instead of having *more* time together, it feels like they have *less* time. Fights arise over long days at work, lack of attention, jealousy, and more. You might have been drawn to their sense of patriotism and service along with their ability to commit to something larger than themselves, but when they've missed dinner, or their training or shift got extended unexpectedly, it's easy to feel like you're not the priority. The sailor or firefighter or officer is doing their job to provide and the one at home is trying to keep things running smoothly, but both partners feel the tension of trying to navigate the new schedule. Both may feel unappreciated and unhappy, perhaps even asking themselves, "Is this what marriage was supposed to be?" Multiply that by any length of time and compound it with additional value clashes, and you've got the making of a disaster.

Start by asking, "What are we fighting about?" or "What am I angry or resentful about?"

It might be time or money or attention or work. Name it and then think about how you viewed it at the beginning of your relationship. If you regularly scheduled dates and outings while dating, maybe you believed that once married, you wouldn't have to put as much effort into it because you'd live together and see each other more. The problem is your time together now includes managing a household even before kids enter the picture, so you don't actually have more time.

Find the core values each of you holds and take time to talk through how your values can better align.

Rediscovering Your Invincible Values

Once you're clear about those initial values that you brought to marriage, you're not quite done. What about the things that pop up only after you're married? Or what if someone changes their mind after they gain more life experience? What if you aren't sure what your values are?

As we said before, values are behavior over time, so it may help to think about where you're going and the culture you want to create and live in as a couple. Part of what drove our values was reacting against some of the drama we saw in our own families growing up. We value unity and respectful disagreement because we saw firsthand what happens when there isn't unity and respect.

You might also look around at couples you know well that have relationship qualities you'd like to emulate. Be careful not to put a couple on a pedestal because no marriage is perfect, but if you see a couple that seems to manage conflict or communication or just do life well together, watch how they are doing it. What choices are they making in the way they interact? How are they prioritizing their relationship, even when things are tough? Finding examples to model can be a way to see what is important for you.

If you've been married any length of time, you've already discovered some friction points. Those places of tension can be a great place to uncover your values and even find ways to compromise to make sure your values align.

For us, a good example of something we had to compromise on was cleanliness around the house. Jason has always been a neat freak, and he wanted order and cleanliness to be a daily priority. The military had only further ingrained that in his values system.

Even when dating, we knew that we didn't keep the house to the same standard. In fact, the one time Jason broke up with Erica while dating, he claimed it was because she was too messy and wanted too much. In reality, he was just scared of the level of commitment marriage required, even though he already knew that if there was someone who could help him navigate that shift, it was Erica.

So it was no surprise that, when we combined households, tension around house cleaning popped up. Erica didn't allow the house to be a pigsty, but she knew with a toddler that keeping a home perfectly clean was a losing battle. It wasn't a priority, and she knew she would get to things when she had a spare moment. Jay on the other hand would come in and immediately feel tense about the clutter of toys or dishes or whatever had accumulated during the day.

This might feel like a small issue on the surface, but your home is where you live the most life outside of work. To have wildly divergent ideas about how to keep it clean and the shared responsibility of that work can really harm a marriage if it isn't done well.

It's easy to pretend that the battle is about cleanliness. It's not. If Jay had come home from work and started immediately criticizing, "Why's the laundry still on the couch?" or "Can't the kids put up their toys?" then we would have been in for a fight because it's likely that Erica hadn't had a minute to herself all day, much less time to finish laundry or dishes.

Instead, Jay learned to think about the long term. How much did it really matter if the house was messy right that minute? Do we really want to expend energy fighting about this? As a result, we found ways to prioritize each other. Jay came home and if the house was messier than usual, he learned to take initiative and put things away if that's what was needed, and not with a door-slamming attitude that he shouldn't have to do it. He sometimes asked Erica how he could help if things were especially chaotic. This created a virtuous cycle; Erica, appreciating his efforts, found little ways to clean throughout the day, knowing that he would appreciate them in turn. His softer approach helped Erica prioritize it more, even during chaotic times.

In other words, Erica made more of an effort to keep things clean and Jay relaxed his standards.

Too many couples approach a small difference like this with anger and hurt feelings. If you've always kept your space clean and organized, it's inconceivable to live differently, and because of that, it's easy to judge. What's so hard about keeping it picked up? How can you live like this? Suddenly housekeeping becomes a weapon you're using to pummel the person who should be your strongest teammate. And that makes both of you weaker in the end.

Compromise starts with a focus on what's truly important, what really matters. And what matters is growing closer as a couple and enjoying life together. Values, when clearly communicated, can help you take a step back to evaluate how to support each other and to avoid picking on each other over smaller issues.

Focus on Team

If you are in a marriage where things have been hard and your values are misaligned, but you want to work at it and stay together, the most important value to adopt now, today, is a team mindset.

You, as a couple, are a team. It should always be WE not ME.

If you've had problems, that might make you uncomfortable. So what? If you decide you want to stay together, then you'll put in the work to become a team. SEAL candidates do twenty-four weeks of intensive training to learn how to become a part of an operational SEAL team, and even then they have to adapt and grow as they work in different platoons, teams, and missions. They are learning to be physically, mentally, and emotionally tough at the same time they learn how to work together under stressful conditions. It takes those elite teams years to learn to operate at the highest levels, but everyone starts somewhere. Why would marriage be any different? This is the most significant relationship of your life. It's work adopting a team mindset and treating each other with full respect and equal priority. As soon as we got married, decisions large and small changed from "me" to "we."

Not too long ago, we were listening to a married friend talk about life.

"Things are great. I've just got promoted at work, and I'm planning a trip down south soon. I've always wanted . . ."

The conversation went on and on, and not once did he use the word "we" despite being married with kids. Every endeavor doesn't have to be shared in marriage, but when you find yourself using the word "I" when you share big changes or decisions in your life more often than you use the word "we," it might be time to check the selfishness and make sure both of you are on the same page.

When you're a team, you have to work together, honoring each other's strengths and covering for each other's weaknesses. In the military, we cover each other all the time. If we're in an urban scenario where threats might emerge from an alley or overhead balcony, we patrol with 360-degree overlapping fields of fire. It means that we cover our assigned area, knowing our teammate is across from us, covering our blind spots. It's a give and take, knowing we're stronger and safer when we depend on each other. That can be tough in the early years of marriage, especially if you didn't have good role models for it. But instead of reverting to old patterns that aren't helping your relationship, start thinking about the two of you as a unit that works best when you're both on board and pointed in the same direction. A team doesn't view their personality differences as liabilities. Jay is intense by nature and tends to run hot when pressed, while Erica is much more laid-back until overwhelmed. Instead of letting those opposite traits drive each other nuts, we have recognized that working together makes us stronger.

When one of you has a setback, it affects both of you, and how you support each other in that moment is critical. If your values align and you know your marriage is a partnership that matters long-term, you'll be sensitive to how you can best support in times of crisis. When Jay made a mistake in Afghanistan that got him sent to Army Ranger school, he didn't want to go—it had already been an extremely challenging time apart. There had been the loss of teammates, the high tempo of training, and combat we'd endured for months. Not to mention the dismal reality that Ranger school meant Jay would be unable to talk or email with Erica and the kids for the duration. Erica was already managing things at home alone with the kids, and here Jason was forced to pay for a mistake with additional training. Erica could have easily been critical—her life wasn't easy on the home front. She could tell Jay was struggling, but it wasn't her battle to fight. But he was her teammate. She never gave up hope that Jay would do what needed to be done and come home again. When he called home angry, frustrated at the situation and contemplating quitting Ranger school, Erica listened, affirmed him, and reminded him she was there for him and loved him, no matter what. Then she trusted him to figure it out. It's not easy to watch your partner struggle through something. You may want to jump in with questions and advice, when often, they need space and support to work through it. Let your shared values guide that needed time, and it will make your team stronger.

A team mindset shifts that "I" thinking to a "we" perspective. Are you looking out for your spouse? Are you thinking about what will help your relationship get stronger?

Action: You Go First

Now that you know how important it is to return to shared values, take a minute to think about what's important to you—don't focus on your partner yet. If you don't know who you are and what you want, there's no way for your partner to align with you.

So, thinking about yourself: **Who do you want to be?** If you see yourself as a parent now or at some point down the road, then that's a value you need to be honest about. If you want to scrimp and save in a high-powered job through your twenties and thirties, living as frugally as possible and aggressively investing so you can retire early in your forties, that's a value. If your faith is important to you, and something you want to share as a family, that's a value. If you're passionate about fitness or Spartan Races or CrossFit, that's a value.

Also, "being happy" isn't a value, but we'll talk about that in our next chapter.

If you're having trouble making a good list, maybe the problem is that you're not living in tune with who you really want to be. In that case, you need to start leading yourself first before you can communicate what you want with your partner. Get honest about how you're spending your time—do a time audit and be brutally honest about where and how you spend your time. You can do this in any number of ways. You could take a sheet of paper and divide it into seven columns (one for each day of the week) and list out the blocks of time: 6–7 a.m. gym, 7–8 a.m. shower and breakfast,

8–12 work, 12–1 p.m. lunch or errands, and so on. You could do it on a spreadsheet or a calendar app. Just start keeping track of how you're spending your time. Be honest. Are you out at the golf course ten hours a week? Behind a video game controller every night for a couple hours? Shopping three days a week even when you don't need to buy anything? Out partying with friends every weekend?

You want the way you spend your time to actively be helping you become the person you want to be. So many people waste time on shit they don't really care about at the end of the day or the end of a life. If that describes you, wake up and make a change.

Maybe as you look at the ways you spend your time, you realize that you're still stuck on old immature habits like mindless scrolling on your phone or binge-watching YouTube or TV. Maybe you find some areas that are completely out of balance like letting your job eat up every hour of your life.

If you're really brave, ask your partner or a close friend what they think is most important to you. If you do this, *do not* get defensive. Shut up and listen to what the person says, asking questions only to clarify, such as, "Hm, what have you noticed in my life that makes you think _____ is most important to me?"

Once you've honestly articulated your own values, spend some time together as a couple talking about how you can better align on the big things. Make a list. Put it on the bathroom mirror or the fridge or somewhere you can both see it regularly. Let it become a part of how you define yourselves as a couple. Just like the SEAL ethos that is posted on the wall of BUD/S training, let those values drive your relationship forward, let them center you when you're facing tough decisions, and know that when you look back, you'll see how your values built the foundation of your marriage.

INVINCIBLE MARRIAGE MOMENT

Values reflect what is most important to you individually and as a couple. When your daily habits and choices are out of alignment with your values, you'll feel perpetually unsatisfied with your marriage and life. Align your core values and begin to make daily choices that support what's truly important to you.

REFLECT

1. Think back to those early days of dating and marriage. Be honest about what you said was important to you in a relationship. Does it line up with reality today?

2. If you had to choose two values that are most important to you personally, what are they and why are they important to you? Share with your partner.

FIRST STEP

Sit down together and discuss the values you each identified. Work to listen as a teammate who is interested in building your partner and relationship up. What do you each need to do to better prioritize and act on your values together? Write those values down and put them somewhere you'll see them every day.

CHAPTER 3

Set Clear Priorities

When we got married in June 2001, we had a fairly traditional ceremony. But there was one element we had a disagreement about: the unity candle. If you aren't familiar, many weddings have a moment in the ceremony where the couple moves to a table where there are three candles: two tall lit taper candles and one usually larger candle between them unlit as the ceremony begins. During the unity candle portion of the ceremony, both partners take one of the lit tapers and they cross them together over the wick of the unlit unity candle, symbolizing the way two lives join together in one flame. Then, traditionally, the individual tapers are extinguished to allow the larger unity candle to burn brightly alone in the middle.

As we planned the ceremony, something didn't sit right, especially the part where we'd blow out our individual candles. Finally, when it was all said and done, we stood there and resolutely held our individual candles, lit the unity candle, and then set our candles down beside it, allowing all three to burn. We'd decided we didn't have to extinguish our individual lights to make the marriage stronger. We were going to keep all our individual fire and build a raging passionate fire between us that made both of us stronger.

Looking back, we realize now how that moment encapsulates how we've made decisions both big and small. We are committed to keeping our individual lights burning, even while we commit time, energy, and resources to our marriage. Even if there are seasons where something takes priority for a little while, we've learned how to communicate through those imbalanced seasons to make sure both of us know we have time and space to grow and the support to do it.

Once you understand your values individually and as a couple, it's time to think about how those look in practical day-to-day operations. Too many couples in our protector communities (military, law enforcement, first responders) find that the day-to-day priorities wreak havoc on their marriages. Ultimatums are thrown around: it's me or the job! And too often, our protectors choose the job. It doesn't have to be this way. Compromise and clear expectations are key.

You may have already discovered a few priorities in the last chapter as you tried to articulate what's important to you. As couples, we often *know* what's important to us, but it's sometimes hard to change the habits that have kept us from working toward that value like we should.

Commitment First

The first priority in any marriage is the commitment to each other: physically, emotionally, relationally, financially, sexually, and every other possible way. It doesn't mean you do everything together, but it means you know your spouse is your most important teammate and whatever actions you take and decisions you make need to build trust into that partnership. One of our newsletter subscribers said it this way: "Your partner can be your everything, but they can't be your everyone." It's back to our unity candle again. You have to keep your individual flame burning, protect the flame of your partner, and in doing that, you will keep your shared bond strong.

This feels like a no-brainer. But it's exactly where many couples lose their way. Why? Because dating often feels like a shared mission, especially once you commit to marriage. You're making time and space for each other, figuring out how to show your partner you love and value them. Then, for some reason, once married, too many couples take a deep breath and sit back, assuming that the work is done. That's bullshit—the work is just beginning. Now, it can be *fun* work. Think about the joy of putting in that extra bit of effort to woo someone in the early days of a relationship. And in a marriage, it's incredible to grow together and discover a richness that isn't even accessible while you're dating. But to get there, you have to prioritize commitment.

As we explained in chapter 1, commitment is both attitude and action. It is a promise to look out for the other person's best interests. After marriage, a lot of couples think they can go back to living the way they did when single or dating, whether that looks like partying, overwork, or just selfishness. Part of why people shy away from commitment or outright resent commitment is because it requires them to limit their freedom in exchange for the greater good. When Jason made his commitment to the Navy and to the SEALs, it meant saying no to a lot of other things—for the greater good. Marriage is the same.

Commitment is a marker of loyalty. There's no faster way to end a relationship than disloyalty and betrayal, and it can be hard to come back from a betrayal because it erodes trust so completely. You can spend years building trust, making deposits in the bank account of your relationship, and drain the whole thing into the negative in one night or moment of bad decision-making. Relationship expert John Gottman speaks to betrayal and how it hurts a marriage:

"An extramarital physical affair is only one type of disloyalty that affects a couple once their sound relationship house falls. Betrayal is fundamentally any act or life choice that doesn't prioritize the commitment and put the partner before all others. Nonsexual betrayals can devastate a relationship as thoroughly as a sexual affair. Some common forms of deceit include being emotionally distant, siding with a parent against one's mate, disrespecting the partner, and breaking significant promises. . . . Betrayal lies at the heart of every failed relationship."

Let's be clear, a betrayal of commitment isn't an accident. It typically starts in your mind long before the actual event. As you let yourself think that quitting is an option, it almost always becomes a self-fulfilling prophecy. Basic Underwater Demolition SEAL instructors drill mental toughness into SEAL candidates because they know that the second you let yourself consider quitting, you're far more likely to tap out. You have to cut those thoughts down in their tracks, root them out and throw them away. If you're frustrated enough by an attitude or action in your partner that the word divorce hovers in your mind, it's time to figure out why that option is even on the table.

If you're at a stalemate with your partner, you may need some help sorting through those feelings—from a counselor or chaplain or other trusted person who can help you look at the situation more objectively. If one of you is building a foundation daily, stacking bricks of commitment, and the other is pulling those bricks down every day, you aren't going to last. Figure out how you can build together by aligning your priorities, and start working together.

For us, we individually think about the actions we take daily in terms of how they will affect us as a team. Some of the small actions that communicate our priorities include a quick text when one of us is at the store, asking if the other needs anything. It looks like checking in with each other during busy seasons, to make sure we're staying connected. It means if one of us has been out of town for the week, we are intentional about time together when we arrive home. If you are making daily choices that don't take your most important teammate into account, you're actively building a future alone. It can start with small things, but those actions cause cracks that quickly combine to create chasms in a marriage.

Here's where communication looks a lot more like action and less like words. You can't start to make changes until you see what's happening right now. Commit to this together and know that you can navigate the other priorities in a way where you both thrive individually and as a couple, even if it's imperfect.

Let's look at one couple who share values and are committed to each other, but struggle to align their priorities.

A Misaligned Couple: Jared and Emma

Jared and Emma have been married for five years. Jared is a Marine, and they've already made three moves since they've been together. With two small children now, and no family nearby, Emma feels like she's handling everything at home alone. Their girls are three and one, and Emma spends most of her time caring for them and taking them to activities or playdates. Her only respite is the gym off base that includes childcare, an expenditure Jared often gripes about because she could go to the one on base for free. Emma tells herself that it won't always be like this. The girls will start school and give them more time as a couple. They'll make more money. Easier days will, eventually, come.

As the Marine Corps Ball approaches, Jared tells her he's bought them tickets and there will be childcare on site for their kids. She nearly cries with relief, excited for an evening in a ball gown alongside her handsome husband in uniform.

"Will you be home by lunch the day of the ball, so I have time to have my hair done?" she asks.

Jared's watching television, but he turns to look at her, and smiling answers, "Of course! I only have to check in first thing that morning. I'll be home the rest of the day to help with anything before we drive over to the event."

Emma makes a hair appointment, and she preps outfits and the babysitting bag to make sure they have what they need for the evening out.

On the day of the ball, Emma watches the clock. By noon, she's texting Jared asking if everything is okay. Her hair appointment is at 1:30, and he'd assured her he would be home by then. When he still hasn't answered calls or texts by 1, she checks with a neighbor to see if she has time to watch the kids for an hour. She isn't home. At 1:25, Emma calls her hairdresser apologizing that she can't make it.

At 2:30, Jared calls. "What's up, babe?" he says.

The relief Emma feels that he's okay is quickly replaced by anger. "I had a hair appointment at 1:30, remember? You said you'd be home in time. Did you have an emergency?"

The line is quiet for a second. "Shit," he says. "I'm sorry. After formation, I did get called to help a Marine over at legal, but then the guys from the squadron texted that they were playing football and invited me. I'm headed home now if it isn't too late."

Emma sighs. "I already had to cancel." She barely hears him apologizing again as she tells him she'll see him home soon.

Emma decides not to let it ruin the evening. It's the first time they've gone out together in months. Jared is still apologizing when he gets home and helps get the girls dressed while Emma does her own hair.

At the ball, they drop the kids off in the childcare room, and Emma takes a deep breath for the first time all day. The atmosphere is celebratory, and she feels a swell of pride as they move from group to group, making introductions and greetings.

That is until a Marine named Will claps Jared on the back. "Congrats on getting the gig in Australia!" Will says. "I'd love a year down there!"

Jared freezes and Emma feels her heart plummet. "Thanks, man," Jared says, quickly excusing them. Emma can't get a full breath.

"What did he mean?" she asks.

"I was going to tell you later. It was announced this morning. I was the only one from our group selected to run a training program in Australia next year. It's such an honor, and it's going to look great when it comes time to promote."

"A year?" Emma sputters. "You'll be gone for a year? Did you know you were up for it?"

Jared ducks his head. "Babe, it's going to set us up for the future. You're always busy with the kids anyway—I didn't think it would be a big deal. This is what you signed up for, remember?"

Emma looks at him in disbelief, but before she can answer, both of their phones ping with texts. Emma looks down and tears flood her eyes. One of their kids has gotten sick and needs to be taken home.

Jared looks at her in defeat. "I can't leave. I'm in the ceremony. I'll get a ride home."

Emma can't even speak. She just nods and turns.

"We'll talk later, I promise," Jared says. Emma doesn't turn around and Jared heads back into the ballroom.

Time

Jared and Emma are in trouble. Their priorities and communication are not in sync. If missing the hair appointment was a one-time miscommunication, then they could bounce back pretty easily. But the failure to communicate and plan together for this major work event that will take him away from Emma and the kids for a year signals a far greater problem is brewing. They've allowed work and kids to take over their time as a couple. We've seen this scenario play out over and over in the spec ops world where guys choose time deployed over being present with their spouse and family. Sometimes you don't have a choice—when the job says go, you have to go—but if you're volunteering for extra time away? There needs to be a conversation with your partner and an agreement on how it's going to work before your name is in the running for selection.

Jared might be right that Emma's time is consumed with the kids, but how are they working together to make sure she has time, activities, and people outside of childcare and household tasks? Emma might be right that it won't always be this way, but is she communicating that she misses their time together as a couple and her need for time for her own interests? Jared might be right that the training opportunity will help him be promoted next year, but why didn't he let his most important teammate in on the decision as soon as he knew he was up for the opportunity?

Time can be one of the easiest priorities to track because your calendar can reveal how you've spent your days to see what's important to you. Jared and Emma are spending time on work and health and family, all good things by the way, but they aren't leaving any time for each other.

How are you making time for each other? You cannot maintain a relationship without time together, even if that time is a daily FaceTime call during a trip or deployment. You are going to grow closer to those you spend the most time with, so choose intentionally. If one of you is spending more time at work than necessary, if that's the priority over your family and marriage, it's time to ask why. If every time you have a weekend off together you're spending it apart on purpose, consider how you're making each other a priority. If you're volunteering for additional shifts or overseas tours that will severely limit the time with your spouse without talking it over first? You're prioritizing something other than your marriage. Make time for each other.

Energy

Energy is a little trickier to measure than time, but no less important a priority. What in your lives is getting most of your attention? Our guess is that it is also taking your energy.

One of the common complaints in marriages is that couples don't see each other until the end of the workday and by then they're too tired for connection, sex, or relationship-building. If you've found yourself in that situation, we get it—especially if you're in a really busy or draining season of your lives. But if you've been in that season for a prolonged period, it's time to make some different choices to make sure you have the energy needed for yourself and your relationship, before you're pouring it out on outside things.

During one of the toughest seasons of our lives when Jason was still recovering from his combat injuries and the subsequent dozens of surgeries, we knew we needed to take time to connect as a couple and a family, so we took a vacation. It wasn't easy but the time energized us as a couple. Recently, we'd been grinding hard on the new business, pursuing a building, and feeling like we were bleeding money, but we knew we needed to get away and recharge our batteries. We spent ten days skiing with the family. It was the longest vacation we'd taken in years. We had plenty of reasons not to go, but we knew we needed to refocus on each other and make sure we had our priorities right. It gave us the rest and energy we needed to come back and press hard into the challenges we'd left behind.

Where does energy come from? At minimum, it's coming from sleep, nutrition, exercise, and mental wellness. But there are other factors as well, including emotions, relationships, and stress management. If you're in a high-tempo job and you spend all day stressed or angry, eating out or inconsistently, drinking after work, and sleeping poorly at night, why are you surprised you don't have anything left to give your partner?

We are in our marriage for life, and we hope to live a long time. That means good habits when it comes to sleep, nutrition, movement, mobility, and stress management. How well are you leading yourself in this area? You can't fix everything at once, but small steps toward building your energy and health can make a big difference in what you have available to give your partner in terms of energy. When couples start dating, they take extra pains to look good for each other, to make specific plans, and to guard their energy so they enjoy the time together. Too many couples abandon that mindset once they are married, and it contributes to dissatisfaction. Make the effort to continue to take care of your body and mind, not just for your own well-being but for the longevity and enjoyment of your marriage.

If your work hours are unpredictable in the evenings, or you're regularly wiped out at the end of the day, try to connect with your partner first thing in the morning. You don't have to carve out hours of time before work, but half an hour to an hour, even just eating breakfast together consistently, will add up in the long run. If mornings don't work for whatever reason, sit down once a week and sync your schedules with time together. Some people think this kills the vibe and spontaneity, but if you haven't made each other a priority, putting it on the schedule can help. Invest the energy in yourself and your partner now for long-term satisfaction.

Resources

One of the other places we often see couples fail to prioritize their relationship is in how they handle resources. It's no secret that money management is an area where couples tend to fight. If one of you is a saver and the other is a spender, and you haven't taken the time to arrange your finances so you each feel like your needs are being met, you're going to go round and round on this fight—maybe for decades.

Even if you have a good working budget and you're in agreement about expenses and income, if one of you starts making changes that cost money, you may find yourself in conflict again. Jared and Emma argued time and again about her gym membership. Jared's right that it costs them more than the base gym, but how often will she realistically be able to use the base gym without childcare? Will she have to hire a babysitter? What will that cost? Emma doesn't know a lot of people in their area yet; a gym with childcare could be a lifeline that allows her to take a deep breath and take care of herself at the same time. But they need to get on the same page about the real costs and benefits of that investment.

We've seen this come up in relationships where someone gets on a health or fitness kick to improve themselves, and it results in significant financial and time outlays, such as a gym box membership, race fees and travel, or nutrition changes and supplements. Some couples struggle when this happens because it may leave one person with more responsibilities as the other devotes more time to the activity or it costs significantly more money. But again, your communication is key. Build up your most important teammate: your spouse. If you're the one on the health kick, discuss it with them and make sure you offer ways to keep it from putting more on their plate. If you're the one watching your partner make these types of changes, ask how you can support them. If you are truly committed to each other first, then anything that requires resources can be negotiated. Just make sure you come to the table and sit on the same side as you discuss and plan.

Invincible Priorities

There are going to be seasons when life's circumstances force a change in priorities. When Jason got shot in Iraq and came home with severe combat injuries, our priorities shifted to full-time managing his care and health. When a specialist had an appointment open up, we dropped everything and made it happen. We knew that we had to make sacrifices to help him heal. When you have an infant or small children at home, they demand a ton of time and energy. When you're in a relationship with someone whose work schedule is unpredictable or relentless, you will have to make decisions about how you get through those seasons as a couple. You can still prioritize your relationship and know that you're going to stand the test of time and come out of it together.

When we were dating, Jason was clear up front that he intended to do twenty years in the Navy. He knew that might be a deal-breaker, but he wanted to be honest. Erica agreed to support that dream. For years, we had to balance the demands of the spec ops world, from its unpredictable training and operation schedule, to the mental toll of combat and worry inherent in that life. As with most things, it's the attitude and approach that will determine whether or not your marriage survives these unpredictable seasons. One time when Jay was deployed, we had a rental property that had needed a new front door, a new washing machine, and a hot water heater repair in the same week (something that all military spouses have experienced), and while it was stress-inducing, Erica made the needed arrangements, letting Jay know what the possible solutions were. When she said things were hard, Jay didn't say, "Look, you knew what you were getting into with my career—it's the priority right now, so just figure it out."

Instead, he empathized when things were tough. So often Erica didn't need him to fix things, but to listen. When he was home, he made sure to prioritize anything that he could to carry more for the family. It was imperfect, but we communicated and gave each other grace and made it through.

This is where Jared and Emma will have to make some changes if they want their marriage to last. Jared made a work decision that would absolutely affect Emma without even having a conversation with her. We're conscientious about keeping each other in the loop in all aspects of our lives. Even in Jay's work-related decisions, he didn't work unilaterally, cutting Erica out of the process. We talked about everything from what orders Jay was taking to what jobs he'd be doing, and it made Erica feel like she was better prepared to support him and understand the unique needs of each deployment cycle—not just the months Jay was gone, but the training workups that happened before each deployment that would make his work schedule unpredictable. If Erica had decided that her business or the kids were her priority above all else, then when Jason needed something, she might have snapped back that she was already doing too much. We didn't take that route. We chose to make our partnership strong first, and to let our priorities flex and bend around that reality.

Is your marriage currently operating as a team where both people feel seen and valued? Do you know what the other wants? Are you thinking about how your day-to-day decisions impact them?

Flexibility is key as you learn to work together. Just because Jay tells Erica he needs to talk to her about a business problem doesn't mean she can automatically drop everything right that moment to listen, but she notes it and makes time as soon as possible to make sure it's addressed.

When Jason gets locked into mission mode and barely looks up from work to stay hydrated or eat lunch, Erica is the one who reminds him to take a minute to give her a hug or take a break. We call these random mandatory moments (RMMs). In that instant, Jason may hate being interrupted, but he always participates because he knows those moments are a quick way to show that our relationship is the priority. If he's absolutely in a place where he can't take a quick break, Erica doesn't take it personally. She'll just try again later if Jay doesn't find a natural place to stop and approach her first. It's the give-and-take that makes us invincible, always assuming the best intent and working toward the greater good for our marriage and life.

Find ways to show each other that you are the priority. That they are your number one teammate, and when you're both pulling in the same direction together, it's amazing how far you can go.

INVINCIBLE MARRIAGE MOMENT

Priorities reflect how you spend your time, energy, and resources. They don't have to become a battleground where you constantly fight when you establish clear expectations and work to compromise together.

REFLECT

1. Revisit the story of Jared and Emma. What do they need to do first? Why?

2. Which of the three priorities feels most out of sync in your marriage right now: time, energy, or resources? How are you communicating those needs clearly and without anger?

3. What is one way your spouse shows you that your marriage is their priority? How are you demonstrating that same priority?

FIRST STEP

Choose one of the priorities that feels most out of alignment and set a course of action for the week ahead. If you've been spending too much time at work, plan an evening home early and prioritize time together. If you've been too tired to connect, find time to go for a walk together earlier in the day or make time to help with household chores that you don't usually manage. Then do it again. Show each other how your marriage is an asset through the priorities you set each day.

PART II

TRAINING

Invincible marriages don't just happen. Once you have a shared mission and commit to each other as teammates, it's time to train and build the marriage you've always wanted, just like SEALs take time to train and bond. From rituals and dreams to mindset and communication, you can build the skills needed to carry your marriage the distance and deepen your enjoyment of each other.

CHAPTER 4

Establish Rituals

The road to becoming a Navy SEAL is arduous. No one expects it to be easy, of course, but very few understand how intense it truly is. As a result, anyone who earns the right to wear that Trident finds themselves in a long line of warriors who have developed discipline and mental fortitude most will never touch—who know what it is to endure pain. That road begins with a formidable screening process and then the twenty-four-week-long Basic Underwater Demolition/SEAL (BUD/S) training. Only 888 candidates were accepted in 2022 for BUD/S, including both officers and enlisted. Of those, they only expected to graduate 175, a 20 percent target that has long been the expected pass rate for BUD/S. It's not just about physical stamina, although that is certainly a part. Far more taxing is the mental game, the ability to continue to push and to refuse to give up, especially when you think you've hit your limit.

Even once you make it through BUD/S, you're not handed a Trident; you need additional training. When Jason went through it in 1995, it required a six-month probationary period of further intense training alongside those who had already earned their Trident. They had to study diving, jumping, weapons, medical, and communications—taking test after test after test. When you finally passed those tests, it culminated with a three-mile swim where you were presented your Trident. When Jason received his, everyone on his team walked by and punched the Trident on him, bruising him in the process, but he couldn't even feel it beyond the absolute euphoria of knowing he'd spent over three years planning, training, enduring, and finally, finally, he would forever be a Navy SEAL.

The process has changed over the years, so some of the rituals are different now, but what remains is the distinction of knowing you have endured a trial very few people in their lifetime will conquer, and you are forever part of a brotherhood.

There's nowhere this is more evident than in the SEAL reunions that happen once a year, including active duty and retired SEALs and their families. The first time Jason attended while still active duty, it was mandatory, and he knew from the moment he arrived he was in for some hazing. He had to drive around some of the older, retired SEALs, but he didn't mind. He ran around with SEALs who had seen and made history right in front of them, from teams that had been in Panama on the tarmac when the team had taken gunfire while completing orders to disable General Noriega's jet to the Mogadishu mission immortalized in the movie *Black Hawk Down* and everything in between. The annual reunions solidify and continue a SEAL culture that spans decades now.

The reunions include families, too, with demonstrations that include the SEAL air and seacraft, skydivers who parachute in, boats that breach the beach, and explanations throughout. It helps spouses and children get a clearer picture of what the SEAL community does as a job.

So, from training to reunion, the SEAL community embraces ritual as a way to cement the SEAL identity and brotherhood. It is a place of belonging, especially important since most people in our everyday lives have no clue about the challenges we've faced in both training and combat. It's a support network as well, deploying help and resources when needed for health and other services.

Marriage is its own kind of training ground, and you benefit from shared rituals. Your marriage might not have a twenty-four-week intensive training course (even if moments feel like it!) but it *is* challenging to learn to live together. If you're not married yet or newly married, it's not too early to think about how you'll regularly connect. Name those nights or activities and pursue them regularly. It doesn't have to be as elaborate as a SEAL reunion; even a Taco Tuesday or Dance Night can become something you both look forward to if done with purpose.

As you're together longer, your anniversary or other life milestones offer the opportunity to celebrate your continued commitment, laughing about the failures of the past and toasting the future. When life feels like it's spinning faster, it can be more difficult to carve out that time, but rituals remind you that you're in this together and still in love.

You may already have a few rituals that you can expand or maybe you need to return to the training phase to create some new ones. Either way, rituals can strengthen your marriage the same way they build the elite fighting force of Navy SEALs. Let's look at why rituals are an important part of a regular training regimen for your marriage.

What Is a Ritual?

The word ritual comes from the Latin *ritus* which means ceremony, habit, or custom. A lot of people associate rituals with religion because some of those customs go back thousands of years and we're used to seeing them depicted on TV or film or even in common experiences like weddings or baptisms. But a ritual can include a baseball player who puts his socks on the same way before each playoff game. It can be a series of activities a family participates in during a holiday or birthday celebration. SEAL rituals include the training and ceremony completed in their initiation to the organization, but they are also in the seasonal and annual events to mark progress and time.

Rituals are about **repetition** and **meaning**. Rituals are typically performed at regular, expected intervals. It can be weekly, monthly, or annually, but the repetition matters. As for meaning, a ritual has some kind of larger meaning embedded in it. On the surface, SEAL reunions might just look like a barbeque with some cool vehicles and skydivers, but the meaning comes from the shared experience—the honor, courage, and commitment to this warrior brotherhood on a larger scale and longer timeline.

In marriage, anything that is meaningful and that is repeated is a ritual. Let's examine why rituals can be a powerful force in your relationship.

Why Rituals?

On the surface, rituals may just feel like pointless superstition. In fact, anthropologist Dimitris Xygalatas began with just that question as he researched his 2022 book *Ritual: How Seemingly Senseless Acts Make Life Worth Living* because he was interested in why cultures across time and space all participate in them. His research found that rituals contain great power. In one interview, he stated, "Rituals help individuals through their anxieties, connect to one another. They help people find meaning in their lives."

His research and that of others suggest that instead of trying to tie rituals to outcomes, we recognize that rituals are opportunities to focus, form meaning or history, and connect—all valuable in building a marriage. You already know this if you're married, because whether you had a huge, extravagant church wedding or stood in front of a judge on a quiet Tuesday afternoon, you likely commemorate that ceremony annually on an anniversary. That's part of why it hurts when one or both of you forget your anniversary. That day was a history marker for you as a couple and remembering it annually is an opportunity to revisit your commitment and connection, in the same way SEAL reunions are a way to remember the past while honoring the tradition that continues.

Before we dive into some of the specific ways you can build better rituals, let's talk about those three areas—history, focus, connection—and how they relate specifically to marriage.

History

Rituals mark time. They are an opportunity to retell your origin stories and to remember what you've come through. SEAL reunions and military ceremonies in general always include both formal and informal storytelling rooted in the past, but those stories and their retelling influence the present and future as well. Each time those stories are told, they invite new SEALs and families into the fold to remind them they are part of something bigger than themselves.

In marriage, it's the same. Your rituals, whether anniversaries or some other significant marker of your history, create continuity. Every time you tell the story of your relationship, you're choosing each other again. You're remembering why you came together in the first place. Sometimes, the retelling makes you realize or appreciate your past or partner in a new light.

Recounting history in your marriage shouldn't fall into an airing of old grievances. You don't have to ignore the tough times to be able to appreciate and recount them honestly. And you don't have to limit it to your wedding story—consider the key memories you've made over the years: the road trip that went wrong, the move that changed everything, the first dog or animal you owned together. Find time to regularly revisit and tell the stories of your lives together. A simple "Remember when . . ." can transform a routine dinner into an informal ritual that strengthens your bond. Your stories, big and small, add up to a rich history that you might be overlooking or worse, forgetting, if you don't take time to remember regularly.

Focus

Rituals provide a sense of focus, something that is especially important when you are under pressure or going through a tough time. Think about the basketball player at the free throw line. They have a specific ritual they follow every time they step to the line, not because the ritual guarantees they always drain the shot but because the ritual returns them to what's important, what they've practiced.

It's easy to get distracted and busy. Rituals keep us from mindlessly plowing through our years without pausing to remember what's important. Not only that, they can actually help us *define* what's important. Rituals themselves can shape how we interact with each other when we share a focus. Just like the SEAL candidates in BUD/S training, those training cycles begin to define what's important in SEAL culture. It strips away distractions.

You don't have to undergo intense physical training like BUD/S to earn that wedding license, but marriage is its own crucible. Rituals can help you find your way back to each other to make sure you're still on course and headed toward the same place. There's a reason a ship's navigator won't let the ship veer off course by even a few degrees. A few degrees over time means completely missing the intended destination. In marriage it's the same. You need to make sure you're not off course, even by a few degrees, because that difference compounds over time. Rituals can provide the focus needed to pull you back on course together regularly.

Connection

True rituals require community and participation, even if it's just the two of you. Because rituals take time, when you participate in one together, it's an opportunity to deepen your connection. You can bet that every time we attend a SEAL reunion, we reconnect with old friends we rarely see elsewhere, but attending it together also gives us new memories. We look forward to it, we plan for it, and we make it a priority.

The most important thing rituals provide in the way of connection is an opportunity for regular vulnerability. When you stop to connect in a ritual way, you invite trust, and building trust together strengthens your marriage. Vulnerability doesn't mean weakness. It means openness, and when you're more open together, it means stronger intimacy, both emotionally and sexually.

Now that we've looked at the way rituals help us through establishing history, focus, and connection, let's look at some specific ways to build rituals and make your marriage invincible. You don't have to do all of these at once. Think especially about what you already do as a part of your relationship that you could lean into first. Then watch for the rituals that would make the most sense for your marriage.

Your Story

When was the last time you told the story of your courtship and wedding? Early in your marriage, you might tell your couple origin story often as you meet new people, begin new jobs, or introduce each other to extended family. But beyond that, it's easy to fall into the day-to-day grind of marriage and not tell that story. You both know it, right? Why tell it again, then?

For lots of reasons! Stories are powerful in our lives and relationships, and the way we frame our marriage story can make or break our relationship. Dr. Daphne de Marneffe's book *The Rough Patch* explores the power of stories that she discovered as a counselor. She found that the most hopeful and connected couples find ways to tell their stories with empathy, respect, acceptance, and even pleasure. If your marriage story doesn't feel like it has all those elements right now, it isn't too late. You can begin to tell your story anew, paying attention to details that emphasize those elements. And no, you aren't writing a fairy tale. But you can be honest and still hear each other out, and choose the highlights. Let's look at a simple example:

Jack and Audrey's wedding day was not the fairy tale they'd imagined. The weather didn't cooperate and several other things went wrong: part of the cake toppled, a dog got loose on the wedding grounds, the band didn't show up after getting stuck in an accident, and it felt like everything conspired against them. On that day, they were both disappointed—not in each other but in the circumstances that dampened the day. They avoided talking about it because the wedding felt like a huge expense that didn't deliver. They are happy enough now, four years in, but they only have one small wedding photo hung in their house, the day was such a mess.

In this version of events, they are choosing to replay everything that went wrong that day. Everything that didn't meet their expectations. But is there potentially a better story they could be recounting about that day?

One question could open up an entirely new way to see and remember their wedding: "While I know a lot didn't go as planned on our wedding day, what DID go right?"

If Jack and Audrey begin to explore and share openly, there might be some opportunities to reframe this story—to still tell their truth, but to bring more empathy, respect, acceptance, and pleasure into it.

Maybe Jack remembers the moment the dog broke loose and the way they froze on the dance floor, looking at each other in disbelief before Audrey fell into laughter until they were both crying. Maybe Audrey remembers Jack rushing to find a groomsman with an acceptable playlist they could blast through the speakers and knowing that while it wasn't what they'd planned, she was thankful to still be able to dance with her new husband. Maybe Jack remembers Audrey taking his breath away the moment she entered the room. Suddenly, this is a much different story—still true, but changed by what they choose to remember and highlight.

As you tell your story, you may realize that there are things you need to take responsibility for. If so, apologize and try to make it right. Maybe in the telling you realize you've been holding on to resentment that isn't productive or fair. Let go of it. It's not going to change the story overnight, but being aware of the ways you've sabotaged or limited your story can open up the freedom to try another version together. Then keep telling that story, and keep emphasizing the parts that bring you closer together.

Annual or Seasonal

Some rituals are best done annually or seasonally. Your anniversary is an easy one, but if it's been a point of contention in the past either because one of you has forgotten or only one of you has been carrying on the ritual while the other just gets to show up each time, maybe it's time to mix it up. If you're realizing you yourself haven't planned an anniversary recently, do one of two things. One, initiate a conversation with your spouse. Apologize for putting it all on them and ask if you can plan the next one. Then follow through. Don't be surprised if there's some uneasiness the first time, since you are still proving that you will do what you say. Just make it happen. The second option is to pick a day other than your anniversary and plan something out. Maybe it's a birthday or your half-anniversary, or the date you met, or some random Tuesday—doesn't matter. What matters is that you tell your spouse you would like to start a new tradition, and you'd like to plan the details. They can just show up and enjoy this year. Then see how it goes. Express your desire to better participate fully together in this annual ritual and go from there.

Some rituals are seasonal. For us, Erica began collecting ornaments during her travels early in our relationship, and we've continued to collect them together. At Christmas each year as we decorate our tree, we get to recount each trip, remembering the fun or disaster that ensued, but always, always laughing together at the life we've built.

Maybe you have traditions around special holidays already. How can you lean into those to strengthen your marriage too? Again, are both of you invested and fully participating in those days? How can you better support each other if those holidays are in fact important to you both? Sometimes couples look at the madness around a holiday and realize it isn't what they would choose together at all, that maybe they are just doing what their parents did or what their friends expected. Forget that. You need to decide as a couple what seasonal rituals will deepen your connection and let the others go, especially if they are draining time and resources from one or both of you.

Some rituals might revolve around monthly patterns, like a special dinner out on the third Friday of each month. For others, if you love baseball, maybe it's tickets to the opening night when your home team plays. Maybe it's not a date but an event, such as the first deep powder on the snow slopes when you cancel everything and head to the mountains. It could be a vacation you take each year to make sure you have time away together. Whatever it is, make sure you both have input, that you both have a hand in planning it, and that you take the time to focus on each other during the ritual.

Weekly Rituals

If you feel like you're just getting started on your ritual journey as a couple, a weekly ritual might feel like too much to keep up with. But you already have things that you do every week, whether it's taking out the trash or filling your car with gas. Those probably aren't rituals that have deeper meaning for your relationship, but they show you have patterns that are a part of how you live. Maybe you already attend a church service together each week or you hit happy hour on Friday night. The question is how can I create one or two small rituals each week to make my marriage stronger? If you already attend a church service together, can you use the time before or after to make it more meaningful together? If you both already fill up your cars with gas once a week, can you go together and hit the drive-through for a milkshake after?

Weekly rituals need to be low-lift. The less planning they take, the more likely you are to repeat them. For us, we often take a bath or get in the hot tub together each week. It's a time when we can be focused on each other, catching up, dreaming, telling bad jokes, and just being together. We've solved problems in our family and business, and more than anything, learned to listen to each other in the tub. It's meaningful to us because we've done it since we dated. Your new ritual can be anything repeatable that you endow with meaning. It doesn't have to have a deep, philosophical meaning. In fact, sometimes the most powerful meaning comes through when you prioritize time weekly together to say, "Hey, I see you, I love you, and we're in this together." Can you add that to something you're already doing?

Weekly rituals may feel harder to do if you're in a tough season caring for young kids, high-needs kids, an intense work season, or aging parents. Those seasons are a huge drain on your time and energy, and we get it. Jason's schedule has always been unpredictable when he was deploying as an active-duty SEAL, but it's still that way now as a speaker.

When we're separated by deployments or work engagements, we're intentional. During deployments, we had weekly calls or emails as much as possible, making sure we asked about the mundane details that made up our days: from the best or worst thing we ate that week to imagining the first place where we'd go to dinner when Jay got home. Communication has to cross the distance if you want to keep your partnership strong. When Jay's away on speaking trips, we text throughout the day. We share what's going well and what's bombing. Even a short text like "I'm thinking about you" communicates love and care.

You can watch the same movie or show during the week and discuss it on your next call. Swap pictures of your location (if it's safe) and play twenty questions to see if you can guess where the other person is. Read or listen to a book together on a topic that interests both of you or in an area where you want to grow. Share your workout regimens to hold each other accountable. Whatever is most important to you, find ways to pursue it as a team.

We still make time to eat together, hopefully as a family, each week whenever we can. In those tough seasons, it is especially important to find weekly time together, because you need each other. It might mean staying up late or getting up early one day a week to sit out on the porch or just in a quiet house holding hands. Turn off the television and figure out one question you can ask each other each week at around the same time—something that lets you share and get vulnerable. For us, we often ask, "Are you happy with our . . ." and fill in the blank. Routine? Family? Sex life? Choose something and get to connecting.

How can you make time together this week? Even fifteen minutes spent well can go a long way toward loving each other better.

Daily Rituals

Daily rituals will change your life faster than almost anything else. When SEALs are in training, there's a reason they are physically challenged every single day. It hones the body and the mind for the arduous work ahead. It can literally save their lives. They don't do exactly the same exercises in exactly the same amounts daily, because as we've said before, the muscles need to be taxed in order to grow. Your marriage is no different.

Start by looking at the beginning and end of the day. How do you greet each other in the morning? What do you do right before you go to sleep each night? Those daily check-ins have the power to foster a stronger connection every single day. Sure, some days you're going to be in such a rush that it's just a quick peck on the cheek before you're off, but if you can prioritize really seeing each other in that moment, it creates a baseline. Don't overlook the power of physical connection daily. A six-second kiss or twenty-second hug have both been found to release oxytocin which helps you feel more connected and secure. Maybe it's sharing a cup of coffee without your phone or a glass of wine after dinner. It could be that your daily ritual is a text sent at lunchtime, alternating between a memory, an appreciation, or a quick I love you. Maybe it's a small act of service like washing dishes together. For us, whoever is up first will bring the other a cup of coffee and we'll sip and discuss the day. Whatever it is, make that repetition *count*. Because those daily moments add up—just like the rituals Jay kept on missions, from gear prep to team checks and communication with home. The repetition ensured success. As author Annie Dillard says about keeping a schedule, "How we spend our days is, of course, how we spend our lives." If we want to be able to look back at our marriage in ten, twenty, fifty years and still be chasing each other around the retirement home, we need to invest in those small daily check-ins that say you matter.

When Ritual Becomes Routine

Ritual is a double-edged sword. On one hand, you have to do them at regular times and intervals to make them effective. Part of what helps you build trust is that dependability. But anything that becomes routine can also become boring. If you aren't paying attention, you'll look up and wonder why the ritual isn't keeping you connected the same way.

Taking out the trash each week isn't sexy. The alternative is a smelly garage, but that doesn't mean you enjoy that ritual. But your relationship rituals shouldn't be approached like a chore.

There are going to be days you don't feel like doing your ritual. There will be weeks you miss due to circumstances beyond your control. But the biggest difference between making your routine a ritual, and making it a chore, is your attitude. Is working on your relationship, honoring it through daily, weekly, seasonal rituals something you *have* to do? Or something you *get* to do? The key is to take ownership of your own attitude and draw on past experiences together to remember why the ritual matters.

Maybe your ritual needs a shake-up. Like a workout routine that is done too often, you need to add some resistance or change to make it effective again. Can you add something new? Change the location? For example, if you always have a date night and it's usually dinner and a movie, switch it up! Go to a trivia night or play cards with friends or do something you used to do when you were dating. If you usually make time for each other in the evening, can you get up early and have breakfast together? Or take a half day off work and go for a walk? It takes energy and intention to keep rituals from becoming boring, but it's also the best way to keep showing each other that your marriage is worth the effort.

If you lean into your commitment and the intention to use your ritual time to make your marriage stronger, you can be creative and switch things up to keep it strong—whether it's a daily coffee date, your sex life, or a seasonal vacation. It's worth the time and effort to keep things fresh and not allow tending to your marriage to feel like a chore.

Invincible Rituals

What are your rituals? How can you deepen the meaning and experience of the ones you already have? Which ones could you add to make your marriage stronger? Whatever you decide, do it together and make sure your expectations are clear to each other. Part of the fun of rituals is the anticipation they create, but that can work against you if one of you expects something different than the other.

Also, make sure that you both take responsibility for your rituals. You can't expect your partner to always plan the vacation, the anniversary, the weekly family dinner, or whatever you've chosen. If only one of you is doing all the work, that's going to breed resentment quickly, and it comes off as only one of you caring about the ritual. Figure out ways for both of you to plan and execute rituals regularly based on your interests and strengths. And get out of your comfort zone if necessary—that expresses your love more than doing something that comes easy sometimes. It's not going to be perfect the first time. Don't be afraid to try a lot of different things until you find the ones that are best for you. Don't be surprised if they shift over time. If you're stealing time after the kids go to bed now, you may find in five years you have more space to take time elsewhere. Communicate and learn to enjoy the rituals together.

INVINCIBLE MARRIAGE MOMENT

Rituals are opportunities to connect and deepen your relationship on a regular basis. Be intentional about daily, weekly, and seasonal rituals to strengthen your bond.

REFLECT

1. What rituals do you already have as a couple? Why are they important to you?

2. Which types of rituals are most lacking: annual, seasonal, weekly, or daily? How could you try one small activity this week to change that?

3. Take time to retell a story or two about when you dated or when you got married. How can you lean into the positive moments you shared?

FIRST STEP

Choose a ritual together and plan out what it will look like. Divvy up the responsibilities. Set a time deadline. Then do it and repeat. Tweak it if needed, but keep after it.

CHAPTER 5

Support Each Other's Dreams

T he fight was almost always about taking vacation. Lisa and Mike are a dual-income couple. They both want kids, but not until they establish themselves in their careers. While dating, they had often gone on adventures, from hiking to road trips to just the regular dinner or drinks at a new restaurant. Before their honeymoon, they'd gone on a couple longer-distance trips: one to Mexico and the other a ski vacation in Colorado.

But since they got married four years ago and bought their home last year, vacation time has been clustered around holidays, almost always with the purpose of seeing their respective families.

They love each other deeply and their values align for the most part. They've navigated those early days of priorities, from communicating about work boundaries to how household chores are shared. But vacation remains a battleground.

At dinner one night, Lisa launches into her newest find, without stopping to ask about Mike's day. She pushed her phone across the table.

"I found this amazing deal on a trip to the Bahamas. Look at everything that's included!" Lisa's face lit up as she talked about the potential trip. "I really think we should go for it."

Mike exhaled, his shoulders dropping. "I have no doubt it would be a blast, but we need to stick to our budget and prioritize saving.

Things have been really slow at work, and I'm worried we won't make our quarterly numbers. We should just meet my parents at the lake like we always do. It's fun, and it doesn't cost us much. Let's put it off just a little longer. It would help if we could cut in some other places too."

Lisa slumped back in her chair, her face pinched. "We can't keep saving every penny without enjoying ourselves. I'm tired of spending every vacation we have with our parents or extended family. When will we have time for us?"

Mike balked. "I'm not saying we can't enjoy ourselves, but we need to be responsible. If you don't want to go to the lake, let's find something else that doesn't break the bank."

"We're putting off living our lives. What's the point of saving so much if we can't enjoy the present? I don't want to wait to travel again together. Once we decide to start a family, it will be harder, and I don't want to wait until retirement." Lisa scrolled through the pics and stopped on one with a couple lounging in chairs on the beach.

Mike ran a hand down his face. "We're not putting off our lives. We're planning for a secure future, and things at work aren't in a place where I can take off for something like this yet. Can we wait and see where we're at after this quarter?"

Lisa tensed. "It's never a good time. Why do I feel guilty every single time I want to plan a trip for us?"

Mike and Lisa have had this argument multiple times, and unless they address what's underneath it, they might be in trouble.

Under the Argument

Do you have some version of this argument circulating in your home? A topic that comes up over and over? It's something deeper than housework that is often about priorities but less foundation-shaking than a misalignment of values about faith or sex. This argument is often future-focused. It deals with competing visions of your future together, whether that's next month, next season, next year, or ten years from now.

There's a rift in your answers to the question, "What's next?" And when you don't communicate, when you don't take the time to dream together, when you're inflexible to change, that question becomes a major source of conflict when it could be a superpower that drives you together and forward as a couple. Do you have dreams as an individual? As a couple?

Sometimes we talk to couples about their dreams or future plans and they shrug and say, "We don't know. We just want to be happy."

Uh-oh. Look, everyone wants to be happy, but it can't be a goal. Happiness is not a dream. It's a byproduct, a secondary result of working toward your shared dreams. In a healthy couple, both partners support and challenge the other to be the best version of themselves. You make each other better. If you've been floating along believing that you just need to save or go on vacation to be happy, it's no wonder you're experiencing everything but happiness.

If you don't know what your dream is—either as an individual or as a couple—think about what you get most upset about. Then start digging. If you're fighting over spending versus saving, ask, What's the endgame here? Why is spending important to you, what does it give you in the moment? Long-term? Or why do you want to prioritize saving? What is the end goal of savings (or vacation or whatever your version of this argument is about)? Instead of setting up finances as a rope between you in a tug-of-war, with each of you on one side, imagine both of you on one side of the rope and your finances on the other—now it's just about pulling in the same direction together. Guess which method is going to actually help you accomplish your dreams and build your relationship at the same time? You've got to get on the same side.

Renowned relationship expert John Gottman calls these recurring arguments "gridlock." He writes, "To navigate your way out of gridlock, you have to first understand that no matter how seemingly insignificant the issue, gridlock is a sign that you each have dreams for your life that the other isn't aware of, hasn't acknowledged, or doesn't respect. By dreams I mean the hopes, aspirations, and wishes that are part of your identity and give purpose and meaning to your life. Dreams can operate at many different levels. Some are very practical (such as wanting to achieve a certain amount of savings), but others are profound. Often these deeper dreams remain hidden while the more mundane ones ride piggyback and are easier to see. For example, underneath the dream to make lots of money may be a need for security."

Whoa. Can an argument about taking vacation really be about unfulfilled dreams? Let's go back to Mike and Lisa's quarrel.

Mike is a saver, a planner. He's good at seeing the big picture and making incremental changes that compound for larger gains in the future. He's willing to sacrifice to stay on track toward the vision he has for their retirement and long-term security. If we asked him to dig into his past, we'd see a childhood that often felt like there wasn't enough—he felt insecure. He doesn't want that for himself or his own family. He's actively working toward that end.

Lisa lives in the moment. She's adventurous and craves new experiences. She hates having to account for and defend every expenditure because she knows that life is short. She lost her dad when she was a kid, and she is comforted by the memories of their spontaneous family trips. She wants to make sure she's making memories that last.

The irony is that those qualities, his stability and her spontaneity, drew them to each other in the first place. But now, after years of being married, it is a source of perpetual tension because they both want things long-term that they haven't been able to properly communicate and adjust to as individuals or as a couple. Underneath their recurring argument about how to spend vacation time and money is a larger conflict related to dreams and identity.

When a Relationship Stagnates

The first problem we can see in Mike and Lisa's situation is one of stagnancy. They are both hard-working, vibrant people, but in establishing their lives together, they haven't engaged the larger question of "What's next?" aside from savings and a family one day. It's not enough, and in the meantime, they've allowed themselves to get stuck.

This happens in most relationships and marriages. As time passes, you settle into routines. That's just part of what your brain wants. It wants the day to be predictable because chaos and constant instability are exhausting to navigate. But predictability can work for or against you. Think about exercise and fitness.

Both of us are health conscious, and we want to stay in great shape long after retirement. We want to be those grandparents out skiing with the grandkids for a long time. We never want our physical bodies to be an impediment to going on adventures together and with our family. Jay lifts weights, while Erica does Pilates, but both of us are pushing to remain healthy. If we did the same three exercises a day at the same weight with the same number of repetitions, it wouldn't matter how consistent we were, there would be limited growth. We have to challenge our muscles for them to grow and stay strong.

Dreams are the same.

If you feel like you're in a rut in your relationship, it might be that you need to mix things up, shift priorities, or try something new as a couple. But it's just as likely you need to explore and communicate your long-term dreams. Dreams are an exercise in imagination—you can't reach something you don't aim for, and dreams can help you envision something beyond your current reality.

From the beginning of our relationship, we shared dreams together. Early on, we often asked, What does the future look like for us? While we were content and happy in the present moment, we knew that what we did in the present would build toward a future. We wanted to be intentional about how we shaped our days to match that future, especially when so much of our time and resources were disrupted by the high tempo of military life and eventually Jay's combat injury recovery. It's really easy to lose sight of dreaming when your daily life is consumed with work or recovery or family obligations. We wanted to make sure that we kept reaching for a future that we'd both love.

For example, when we were dating, we discovered that we both loved to scuba dive. Erica had an idea for a dive bed-and-breakfast to combine the things we loved. We wanted to create a high-end Airbnb rental home experience near water where guests could enjoy the house along with water recreation. In college, Jay put together a whole business plan for the idea in the Florida Keys called Dream Waves, outlining specific goals and the year-by-year projections. That dream would shift and change, but it did several things for our relationship that we likely couldn't have even voiced at the time.

That dream gave us a shared goal that looked beyond our current circumstances. We had kids from the moment we got married, so we needed a dream that reached past those early days that were consumed by training, deployments, and busy preschoolers. At the end of particularly busy days, Dream Waves felt like a life raft, an escape that helped us remember that we would be together and thriving long after Jason's military career ended and our kids had left home. That dream kept us going when things were tough.

That's why happiness can't be your goal. Of course, we all want to be happy, but as a goal, it's not concrete. You can't see it and reach for it. It's best experienced in the moment, and usually when you least expect it. You can be happy even when you haven't fully realized a dream if you are actively pursuing it together.

The Importance of Individual Dreams

Stagnation can also happen individually. All of your dreams can't be bound up in your identity as a couple. You need individual dreams as well, and then you need to be supporting each other toward those dreams. Even when you don't get it.

Jason's dream was a military career, and it was something we agreed to support together from the beginning. Jason always said the first twenty years were for him, and after that, Erica could decide how much longer we stayed on active duty. Combat injuries dictated the end date, but Jay was able to complete his dream of a military career as a Navy SEAL. Erica fully supported his dream, even when it resulted in time apart, injuries, pain, and long-term challenges.

But Erica had numerous individual dreams too. Jay was deployed in Afghanistan at one point in our marriage, and during one of his routine calls, Erica was so excited that it felt like the line was vibrating.

"I want to raise and sell Bengal cats," she said.

Jay waited on the line, unsure he heard her correctly. "What's a Bengal cat?"

"They are domestic cats with these beautiful spotted markings, like a leopard. It's a really profitable business! I want to get started on this," she said.

Jay loved hearing her passion, but he was still thousands of miles away in a combat zone. She was back in Virginia with the kids trying to manage the household and kids' school and activities.

"Look, I don't think it's the right time. Can we talk about this when I get back?" Jay said, hoping secretly that it would pass before he got home. He didn't have anything against cats, but it sounded like a lot to take on at home. Erica agreed to discuss it further when he returned.

When Jason came back stateside, Erica said she'd talk to him about the Bengal cat business once he'd had time to rest up. The day came, and Jay sat on the couch ready to listen. Erica came in dressed in a business suit, with a laptop under her arm, ready to go. Erica had prepared a full PowerPoint business plan, with full outlay of startup costs, projections, photos, and the selling points. She'd turned her dream business into a specific plan with a roadmap for accomplishing it. Long story short, we owned a Bengal cat breeding business for a while and it did well.

Both of you need individual dreams in addition to the ones you share together. Why? You have unique gifts, personality traits, desires, aspirations—all of them borne out of your experiences and identity. You need a place to let those run wild. If only one person in the relationship is pursuing dreams, the other will likely feel resentful that they're always holding down reality while their partner tries to fly.

You have to feel fulfilled as an individual to be the best you can be as part of a couple. Some couples make the mistake of going all in on only one person's dream—maybe it's a military career like

Jason's or a doctor who is going to spend a long time in training before it begins to pay off financially. Maybe one person has a dream to complete some high endurance race or mountain peak that takes hours and hours of time each week and family resources to fulfill. If only one of you has a dream, the other is going to feel left behind sooner or later.

Be intentional about making sure you have a dream, that you're dreaming big and it's aligned with who you are and where you want to go. If you aren't sure, look back to those recurring fights like the one Mike and Lisa have about saving versus vacations. Part of the reason they continue to have this fight is because they haven't been clear about their individual dreams, and the pursuit of those dreams.

They need to go beyond a big bank balance or a week in the Bahamas and really delve into what those goals say about their respective dreams. They need to ask themselves individually what's next for me, and then they need to find ways to communicate and support each other in those endeavors.

Problem: Lack of Communication or Support

Communication is key when it comes to individual and shared dreams. You can't support each other if you haven't communicated about the end goal. Sometimes couples don't communicate because they aren't sure what their dreams are. Sometimes it's because they're scared their partner won't support them. Other times, they just haven't seen good models of how to communicate effectively. Whatever the case, you can learn to communicate your dreams and learn to support each other.

Here's where you need to return to that team mindset about values we discussed in chapter 2. The highest value is for you to be a strong team. If only one person is talking all the time, and the other is doing all the listening, it isn't a partnership. Both of you have to take responsibility for your part in sharing your dreams, concerns, and support.

When we talked with Dr. Gabrielle Lyon and her husband Shane Kronstedt, they embodied this shared responsibility for each other's goals and dreams. Already a doc, Gabrielle knew what it was going to take for Shane to do med school and a residency, and she said, "I want him to be successful. My expectation is that he's going to be amazing. I want to fully support him. He settled me. He's my teammate who is steady, anchoring, and available. It allows me to operate in safety that I haven't had before." They are incredible teammates and each other's biggest supporters day in and day out because they keep the long game in mind: they are both passionate about using medicine to help people.

Let's look back at Mike and Lisa's argument. They stay focused on their own feelings and don't call each other names or minimize the other's experience.

But they also stay on the surface. The recurring fight is about vacation versus savings. Interestingly, both of them agree that vacation and savings are important values and priorities, but they disagree about how to balance them. They seem to believe it is one dream or the other. Think again about that tug-of-war rope. They've each taken up one end, believing that only one can win, when that's not true. Looking at their dreams and better understanding the motivations behind what they each want can get them back on the same side of the rope.

One salve for gridlock is curiosity. What if one night, in the midst of this argument, Lisa were to say, "Tell me about why saving feels so important for you. When did you first know that you wanted to make sure you were financially secure?"

Then Mike could ask Lisa what she loves most about vacation with him and what made their Mexico vacation so particularly relaxing and fun. He might ask about her favorite adventures growing up. No matter who broaches the subject and tries to turn toward longer-term thinking, both need to commit to listening and really understanding what the other person says.

When Erica wanted to start the Bengal cat business, Jay chose not to intentionally say things that would discourage or set Erica back. This can be especially challenging if your parents threw language bombs at each other. You're going to have to stop and think before you say things you can't take back—things that will resound in your partner's mind for a long time. Like threatening divorce, once it's an option, it's hard to take back and it becomes a kind of self-fulfilling prophecy. The way couples talk to each other can do irreversible damage.

Once you find your way to the heart of the issue, you can begin to find ways to support each other's dreams. For Mike and Lisa, it might mean reworking their budget to make sure they take time to make intentional memories on adventures that satisfy Lisa's spontaneity and Mike's commitment to staying on steady financial ground. If Lisa is feeling stifled in her job and wants something that embraces more risk, it may be that a new business venture can help her satisfy that aspiration and part of her identity. If Mike's pursuit of stability is stemming from feeling like things at work are precarious, then Lisa can better understand why this might not be the best time for an extravagant trip but that it might be the perfect time for something a little cheaper and closer to home.

There are so many ways to approach their gridlock once they see the underlying reasons those positions are important to them. And dreams, both those as individuals and those they share as a couple, can keep them moving forward together in a positive direction in the meantime.

Remember that you don't have to understand your partner's dream to fully support it. There were so many times during Jay's military career that Erica didn't fully understand why he was pushing in certain directions, but she remained his biggest cheerleader. Right before Jay was scheduled to deploy for the first time after he became an officer, he got infectious colitis. He was furious, adamant that he needed to deploy or everything had been wasted.

"None of this matters if I don't get to the combat theater and prove it on the battlefield," he said, disgusted that he had to wait for a colonoscopy and thirty days of medical clearance to join his team.

Erica knew he was a formidable warrior even without stepping foot on that particular battlefield; he'd already done so much in his career. She couldn't see how this was more than a short setback, but she didn't minimize his frustration. She remembered his long-term dream of a military career, and the steps he'd taken to graduate and get commissioned, and she reassured him that he would get cleared and would be able to join his team. She supported him instead of complaining that their lives were again on hold due to complications with his job.

When Erica pursued the Bengal cat business, it wasn't Jay's dream, but he supported her by asking how he could help and taking action to make it happen. He devoted time and interest to her ideas, not because he cared about the cattery but because he loved her and wanted to support his most important teammate.

Choose to support each other in dreams both large and small.

Problem: Lack of Adaptability

The last thing you need to be prepared for when pursuing dreams is change. Some dreams are going to change over time, even if you pursue them wholeheartedly, even if you've communicated them like a rockstar, because change is inevitable. Life is going to throw unexpected circumstances your way. You can't expect to be rigid and survive. Knowing that your dreams are flexible will actually make you stronger as a person and a couple.

Our goals have changed over the years more times than we can count. When we were still in the military, we talked about what military retirement might look like. Beyond the dive bed-and-breakfast, we looked at farms in Kentucky, and we had a vision for how we'd live on a piece of property outside Louisville, to raise more animals like peacocks, miniature cows and horses, and other livestock. For a time, we planned to own an RV and travel across the country. Now we're looking at condos in areas where we love to ski, so we always have a place to gather with our kids as they are grown with families of their own. Our dreams have always had room to grow and change.

With Mike and Lisa, it's clear from their discussion that they once agreed about their savings goals. But at some point, Mike or Lisa (or both!) clearly questioned or shifted those goals in their minds. It's time to have a conversation about what has changed and why. Because they're fully committed to each other, Mike will hopefully listen and work to compromise in ways that make both of them feel like they're on the same team. Mike doesn't want his need for savings to stifle the fun-loving spontaneity of his wife— the very quality he noticed and appreciated in her when they were dating. Lisa hopefully can affirm the sensibility of being financially secure, which will enable them to have adventures together for years to come.

A relationship often starts out with mutual ideas and dreams of what a couple wants, but eventually people give up, they settle, instead of letting dreams evolve. Other times, rigidity gets in the way.

As we write this book, Jay is training for a swim in New York later this year. With Jay, it's impossible for him to half-ass anything, so he's been extremely regimented in his training, his nutrition, and his schedule in preparation for this swim. Erica is no stranger to the all-in cycles that mark Jay's pursuit of his goals. His method is marked by a strict adherence to his regimen and intense attack both mentally and physically.

Erica approaches her fitness goals in a much more balanced way. She doesn't deprive herself of a glass of wine or a slice of pizza, even as she keeps her objectives in clear sight.

Both of us support each other in the end goal, but also in the approach. Jay doesn't try to force Erica into training like he does, and Erica lets him live in his intense bubble of preparation, even if she thinks he could stop and have a glass of wine with her once in a while. We've both accepted that we approach our goals a little differently, and that's okay. We love each other and trust that if one of us wants feedback or help, we'll ask. There's a give-and-take that we accept to make sure we keep the end state in sight. There's such a difference between setting ourselves up against *each other* and setting ourselves up against the *problem*. We choose to stay on the same side of the rope, even if we have different techniques in the way that we pull.

Leave enough room for yourselves and your dreams to grow. Keep checking in with each other to make sure the dreams and goals you've discussed haven't shifted. When they change, embrace each other and a new direction when you can. Dreams can keep you excited and motivated, moving in the same direction with purpose, and as a result, you may just find that purpose and direction results in the byproduct of happiness. So, what's next?

INVINCIBLE MARRIAGE MOMENT

You need dreams to keep your marriage from stagnating. Communicate those dreams clearly with each other and leave room for them to adapt and change over time.

REFLECT

1. Think about the argument Mike and Lisa had about vacation. What were each of them missing? How could they resolve it?

2. What is your dream? What is your partner's dream?

3. How well are you communicating about your dreams, both personal and shared?

4. How flexible is your dream? How might you be able to reimagine it?

FIRST STEP

Have you given yourself permission to dream as individuals and as a couple? Block off a period of time and label it "Dreams." Then sit down together during that time and talk about the question, "What's next?" What dreams do you have individually? As a couple? Don't feel locked in—make a big list together and see how it feels to think beyond your current circumstances and life stage.

Then choose one or two things to chase, even if it is in the smallest way imaginable. Set aside time to research what you'd need to pursue the dream, make a business plan, whatever your small steps are that make that dream begin to feel more real. Then pursue it together, creating regular quarterly check-ins, remembering and expecting that a dream might shift over time.

CHAPTER 6

Adjust Your Mindset

You'd think the greatest test to our mindset as a couple would be Jason's long recovery after his combat injuries almost took his life. Erica came into Bethesda that day resolved to be strong and positive enough for us both if needed. Luckily, Jay's indomitable, never-quit attitude had survived the enemy ambush. There were frustrating moments, sometimes weekly, but we knew what had caused the damage to Jason's body. We had teams of doctors, surgeons, therapists, nurses, and other specialists who created a (mostly) clear treatment plan for putting Jay back together. Even on really hard days, we knew on some level what to expect from each phase of his treatment. We just had to stay committed to each other and the treatment plan.

So, you'd think nothing else could test the positive mindset we'd developed and depended on as a couple. You'd think that traumatic experience would establish a baseline that couldn't be shaken. But you'd be wrong.

In the fall of 2020, Jason's health had taken an odd turn and not because of COVID-19. He was exhausted to the point where he couldn't make it through a virtual speaking engagement or a podcast recording. We started adjusting his schedule. If he had a podcast interview, we had to clear the rest of the day, so he could go back to bed. He could make it through an hour-long talk if he was able to sit, but then he needed an entire day to recover.

Over and over again, his heart was racing, he had shortness of breath, and it was just so out of the ordinary that he'd text or tell Erica, "I need to go to the hospital." Sometimes it was localized numbness—an arm suddenly out of commission or a leg. Other times Jason felt his throat closing like he was having an allergic reaction. More than anything else, persistent fatigue plagued him. It was unnerving for a guy who normally had the energy of three men.

Hospital visit after hospital visit, doctor after doctor, no one could offer a diagnosis. His blood had abnormalities, but there weren't markers for cancer or other debilitating diseases. For six months, it felt like a Russian roulette of physical impairments were taking turns assaulting him. In the span of two months, he lost forty pounds, and developed anxiety and panic at the loss of control in his body, the one area he used to be able to bend to his will without fail.

Erica was frustrated alongside him, but deep inside she felt like he was exacerbating the physical symptoms with his anxiety spirals and deep dives into WebMD. She never doubted he was sick, but the unpredictability of his symptoms and daily condition wore her down. It wasn't just our marriage and family life—Jason was the center of our business. If he couldn't speak, and be up front on social media, we worried we would lose it all. Behind the scenes, we shored up what we could on his good days and searched for answers that might restore him to some semblance of normal.

Through it all, the question hovered in our minds: Is this purely psychological? And if it is, how can we deal with the causes to lessen the impact?

It was a daily battle. In April 2021, Dr. Gabrielle Lyon found a parasite that was partially responsible for his symptoms—something he probably picked up during his time in South America decades earlier that had sat dormant for years. Jay started a medicine protocol to get rid of it.

By May, his symptoms were improving but not entirely under control, until we finally got a diagnosis that completely explained the gauntlet of symptoms Jay had been battling for months: pernicious anemia. Pernicious anemia is a condition where the body can't process and use vitamin B_{12} like it needs to. Jay started treatment for the anemia and began seeing improvement.

That spring, we traveled to Boston to see a specialist. We were there for medical appointments, but we were staying in a touristy area. One day it was pouring rain and brutally cold with forty mph wind gusts. We were trying to get some groceries. Erica had brought the wrong shoes, so she was in flip-flops and one of the places where we tried to go in to get groceries had asked us to leave because we had Jay's service dog Kharma with us, despite Kharma wearing his service vest. We were both miserable, cold, irritable, and as we crossed a bridge just trying to get back to the hotel, our umbrella caught a gust of wind and turned completely inside out.

At that moment, the tension and frustration that had pent up for days, maybe even months, dissolved between us as we doubled over laughing. If we didn't laugh through it, we'd cry—or worse, take it out on each other. We chose to laugh.

The pernicious anemia diagnosis relieved the tension of uncertainty that had hovered over us for months, and the treatment began to work. Slowly, Jason regained his strength and body weight. But that year had shaken us in a way we weren't prepared for. It was a good reminder that successful couples don't coast—complacency and taking things for granted can upend progress and your relationship just as quickly as fighting.

The Problem of Complacency

Complacency begins with feelings of satisfaction and comfort—such a weird phenomenon that the very place danger begins is the same place you feel like you've been trying to get to all your life. You get good at something, and you begin to rest on your past performance and assume the results will continue to emerge without further effort or growth. When things are going well, it's easy to want to coast. We want to sit back and enjoy what we've built, right?

There's nothing wrong with enjoying success and contentment. It's probably essential. But you can't live there. We have a saying in the military: complacency kills. Complacency causes warriors to get lax. They stop paying close attention because it feels like they can rely solely on muscle memory. They might get a little cocky in thinking that they can do this with their eyes closed. And then they're hit with a curveball—and in military life, one mistake can be deadly. We're not saying you have to stay on high alert like you're in the crossfire all the time. That's hell on your nervous system and not healthy. But you can't coast and expect to have a vibrant, growing marriage. If the things you did to get to a good place in your marriage aren't working the same anymore, what changed? The ironic answer is this: nothing changed, and that might be the problem.

Think about it. How many times have you heard yourself or others in a marriage say something like, "We used to . . . but it's not the same anymore." Whether it's sex, vacations, dinner, household labor—whatever the issue, it might be that you've allowed that area to stagnate. You've become complacent.

It's easy to understand why it happens. Once the wedding is over, you actively try to settle into a daily rhythm, so there isn't so much friction. Other areas of your life, like work or hobbies or friends, may have taken a back seat to your courtship, and now you're trying to balance things a little better. Your time is finite though, so when you start pouring time and energy into things outside your marriage, without keeping any in reserves for your partner, you're going to slip into complacency. And that's a danger zone.

Jay's health concerns were so disorienting for us because he had always been able to drive through things physically—even when he was recovering from combat injuries. We took that ability for granted. We had never been put in a place where we had so little control for such an extended period of time, especially when no one had answers.

The truth is that you can't control everything. You probably have less control than you think over most of your life. But what you do control is your own attitude and response to whatever comes your way. You control how highly you prioritize your marriage, and whether you continue to nudge each other to grow and keep things fresh and exciting. So, how do you do that? To adjust your mindset and make your marriage invincible, do three things: own your stuff, resist the lie complacency tells, and practice positivity.

Own Your Stuff

When things feel like they've changed (or haven't changed), it's easy to start the blame game. As Jay battled fatigue and anxiety, it was so out of character for him that Erica had a thought in the back of her mind that his symptoms might be psychological—that Jason needed to get more rest, get back to his healthy habits, and somehow find a way to get his mind to stop working overtime. Luckily, she never said any of those things out loud, but in many relationships, it's easy to cast blame first.

Let's look at a common example. Marco and Brandy often have tense discussions about household chores. Marco works a lot of overtime, and Brandy, while grateful, feels like more often than not, Marco leaves all the household chores to her, even the ones he's agreed fit in his schedule. When he forgets to put the trash on the curb for the third week in a row, the fight that has been simmering explodes the moment Marco gets home after a long day.

"You forgot the trash again," Brandy states flatly.

"Jeez, I'm barely in the door. Can't it wait a minute?" Marco says.

"No. It can't. We have a stinking pile of trash out back because you've said over and over again you'll get to things in a minute. It's not too much to ask for you to put the trash out each week. I do everything else." Brandy's arms are crossed, and anger has made her face red.

"Everything else? Is that what you think? You don't appreciate how hard I work for us. It's just trash. You're nagging me all the time when I just need a little downtime. You used to be so fun to be with. Where'd that girl go?"

The color drains from Brandy's face. "I guess she's been lost trying to manage this household alone. You don't care about us or our home anymore." She stomps off.

Blame is rooted in defensiveness. If I can blame you for ignoring our budget or being on your phone during dinner or staying late at work when you agreed to be home, casting the responsibility on you, it makes me feel like I'm doing all the things needed to make the relationship work. It lets me off the hook. But if both of you are blaming each other and getting defensive and combative every time an issue arises, you can imagine how well you'll resolve conflict. You won't.

Part of why blame is so insidious is that it quickly devolves into attacking character. When did Brandy switch from blame to an attack on Marco's character? When she said, "You don't care about us." Marco shifted from the problem of trash to a character attack when he equated her wanting to get the chores done with "not being fun anymore."

If someone consistently forgets to put the trash on the curb on trash day, it can build to a place where the attack comes out as, "I can't count on you to help with this. You're so irresponsible." And now the trash-forgetter is on the defensive and feels like their partner doesn't see all the ways they *are* being responsible.

There's no positive way out of the blame game, since it's rarely only one person's fault. So how can you avoid the blame game whether the original issue is complacency, feeling taken for granted, or outright conflict? You have to own your stuff.

Own your stuff means that you honestly examine what you are bringing into your relationship daily. Spend as much time examining your own actions as you do thinking about your partner's. When an issue pops up, don't let it simmer—own your part of it and ask how you can work together to fix it.

With Marco and Brandy, imagine if, when Marco had forgotten the trash the first time, he had owned his mistake and taken steps to rectify it.

"Oh babe, I'm sorry. I was running late today and forgot. How about I run our bags to the dump tomorrow after I get off? And I'm going to set a weekly reminder in my phone."

If Marco had done that after the first or even second time, and followed through with his actions, this would be a nonissue.

Now let's think about Brandy, because she could have approached this better too. What if she'd said, "I know you're just in a really busy season at work. You're not forgetting on purpose. Would you have time to take our bags to the dump this week, so it's not building up? Could we set an alarm on your phone for the night before or is this something that you'd rather I take on and you can pick up one of the other chores that falls on a better time for you during the week?"

Now Brandy has approached the problem with a team mindset. She's owning that maybe this chore isn't on a good night for his schedule and that they need to renegotiate. Notice how in these revised responses, no one is casting blame, and both are coming at it from a team mindset. Our guess is that no one is going to bed that night fuming about trash.

Resist the Lie

Complacency can feel like you're being taken for granted, and that can make you abandon your never-quit mindset and the commitment you've pledged to your marriage. You promised to stick it out through thick and thin, and now you can't even handle a disagreement about the trash or the frequency of sex or who's running the carpool?

Of course, your disagreement isn't only about the trash or sex or carpool. It's about unmet expectations, and when you feel neglected, hurt, or angry, it's easy to create a story about your partner that isn't true. When you're stuck in this loop, it's like your brain starts playing a game of make-believe. You start creating these stories about your partner, like a defense mechanism. It's your mind's way of trying to make sense of why things aren't adding up the way you thought they would. These stories, though, can be way off base, filled with assumptions about your partner's intentions, feelings, or even their whole personality. The tricky part is, these narratives you're spinning might have nothing to do with reality. And here's where it gets even messier. Thanks to complacency, you might find yourself projecting your own feelings onto your partner. Let's look back at Marco and Brandy.

If Marco's working crazy overtime, Brandy is likely already feeling neglected. Marco is probably feeling disconnected from her because of all his time away from home. Instead of realizing they're just swamped, Brandy might start thinking Marco's intentionally ignoring her and the household needs, like he doesn't care.

He assumes all she cares about is the house and accuses her of not being fun anymore. These assumptions, if you let them hang in the air, can turn into a full-blown cycle of misunderstanding. When both of you are working off of false beliefs about each other, the real issues get lost in the mix. It's a recipe for relationship chaos.

Marco and Brandy's main problem is a lack of time together. When they only make enough time to high-five in the kitchen over household duties, of course they both feel neglected, ignored, incomplete. If we backtracked with them to when it began, we'd likely find that the first week Marco took on more hours at work, he thought things were good enough at home to withstand a little more time at work. Brandy may have even encouraged him. But over time, hour by hour, they've lost connection, and no attention to chores is going to fix that chasm.

That's why it's so important to be vigilant about the stories you're running on repeat in your head, especially related to your partner. Watch for words like "never" or "always" in your thinking (or speaking!). They almost always reveal overgeneralizations:

"You always forget to take out the trash" or "You never initiate sex anymore."

To combat the lie complacency wants to tell you about your partner, you need to notice when you shift into assumptions—and combat them directly. When Erica worried that Jay's health concerns might be mostly psychological, it might have been easy for her to say, "This is just in your head, we're always going in circles about your health, why can't you just power through like always?" She actively resisted that thinking. She didn't even let it cross her lips. Why? She is committed to Jason fully, and she knew that such accusations would not only hurt Jay and their relationship, but that kind of negative assumption might make the situation worse. So, what replaces the lie? Practiced positivity.

Practiced Positivity

Instead of believing the lie that complacency sells, we practice positivity. Not a blind optimism that glosses over issues and just believes everything will work out without any effort. That's not optimistic, that's delusional. Practiced positivity is a choice that fully sees the challenges in the moment and still says this commitment is worth it and we can get through it together.

When Jason arrived in Bethesda in 2007 with life-threatening combat injuries, he dreaded seeing Erica. On one hand, he wanted to see her so badly he could taste it, but he didn't want *her* to see *him*. He had tubes running out of every part of his body. His face was blown out from a machine-gun round, his arm wrapped with his elbow destroyed. He wouldn't be able to hold her against his chest with both arms. And he knew the stats. He knew how many spouses didn't show up after a combat injury. He knew that the trauma of long-haul recovery had ended so many marriages.

But when Erica came through that hospital room door, there was no trace of distaste or fear at the sight of Jay in the hospital bed. She said we were going to be alright, and she made good on that promise every day of Jay's recovery.

Were we optimistic? Yes and no. Jay was in rough shape and he had a long road ahead of him, but Erica also knew that they already had a foundation that had been tested by other challenges. She knew that they would depend on each other and keep each other strong. She let their past perseverance inform her ability to stay fully positive in the moment. Does that mean she didn't have any tough days? Of course not. But over and over, she chose positivity. Negativity wouldn't help Jay heal, and it wouldn't benefit their relationship. So why waste time with it?

Part of what can help you practice positivity, especially when things are tough, is understanding how to communicate to counter both complacency and negativity. It's the difference between raising an issue respectfully, with a focus on solutions, versus resorting to criticism.

Criticism is negative. There's almost no way to give it without also delivering a sting of negativity. It's also other-focused, meaning you're delivering criticism to your partner for something *they* are doing. If you shift from criticism to raising issues respectfully, now you're not on opposite sides of the table. You're on the same side trying to find a solution.

We had to learn that sometimes Erica just wants to process an issue out loud without being fix-it focused. Jason had a steep learning curve in this area because he's so action oriented and solution focused, in part because of his time and training in the military. But some problems need to be explored fully before any other steps are taken. Erica raises those issues in ways that begin with how they're affecting her. She doesn't expect instant, quick fixes; in fact, we've learned to resist those easy Band-Aids and to make sure we're moving forward in the same direction for the long term.

It goes back to considering the desired end state. If you want to be a strong team, it does no good to tear each other down on your quest to address an issue. So find something positive, outline what's happening objectively without pointing fingers or casting blame, and realign your expectations.

When you believe the best about your partner, when you look for ways to stay instead of ways to leave, you can face any obstacle together.

Control What You Can Control

If complacency rises out of comfort leading to a lack of effort, and that results in unmet needs, it won't be enough to just resist the lie your brain is projecting. You're going to have to do something different—take action that counters that negative mindset.

Too often, when a couple's relationship feels chaotic or disconnected, the action one or both partners take is to isolate themselves further. It's a protective measure, but ironically, it doesn't actually protect you. It makes your relationship even more vulnerable.

Instead, reach for empathy. Try to see the situation from your partner's point of view, even if you're so angry you can barely see straight. It's going to take time to shake things up and get out of the complacency, negative-assumption loop, but the very first step out is empathy.

You probably know more about your spouse than you think. Everybody is wired differently, and if you've trained well and paid attention at all during dating and the early days of marriage, you've likely already noticed what makes them tick. What times of day are they at their best? What helps them relax? What sets them on edge? Use that knowledge to understand why they are feeling the way they are. If you can't imagine what something feels like for your spouse, ask them! In fact, that curiosity may open an opportunity to get to the heart of whatever has been eating away at your connection. As you have an honest conversation, focus on what you can control, not on what you can't.

Even in the midst of his exhaustion in 2021, Jason often looked at Erica and apologized. He couldn't control the illness, but he hated that it was happening to them and he could control how he expressed that to her. He would say out loud, "I'm sorry this is happening. You don't deserve this."

Just his recognition of the difficulty we were facing lightened the load for Erica. She reassured Jay they were still in it together, that if he was suffering, she was suffering, and we would get through this, just like every other challenge. We took it as it was, tried to focus on the positive things and deal with the negative. What we couldn't control we didn't stress over. We refuse to be driven by anxiety.

Jay's recognition was also a kind of gratitude. Don't underestimate the power of appreciation in your marriage. It's like adding a secret ingredient. Say thanks for the little things, recognize each other's efforts, and keep a regular check on those expectations. Adjust them as needed. Creating a culture of gratitude and growth is the name of the game. That way, unmet expectations become chances for you both to get each other even better, instead of becoming sources of disappointment.

The Invincible Marriage Mindset

To be truly invincible, stop thinking marriage should be easier and look at the obstacles as regular opportunities to resist complacency and grow your commitment to each other. If you get on the same page before issues arise, you can even work out inside jokes that can diffuse even the tensest situations, like our laughter on that bridge in Boston or our running joke about when it's too late to run. Any challenge we face will just be one more story in the thousands about our marriage.

INVINCIBLE MARRIAGE MOMENT

Any obstacle you face in marriage is an opportunity to resist complacency and grow. Resist the temptation to blame or be defensive and work together to control what you can and to lean on each other with practiced positivity that your relationship can go the distance.

REFLECT

1. Look back at the story of Marco and Brandy. How could they resolve the issue? What do each of them need to own or change?
2. In what areas have you gotten complacent in marriage?
3. Where is negativity telling a story that isn't entirely true?
4. How difficult is it for you to maintain a positive mindset in the face of obstacles? What can you choose instead of negativity?

FIRST STEP

We established that complacency comes when you are comfortable. Get uncomfortable this week together. Try a new workout or physical challenge. Learn about something new that interests you both. Have sex at a different time or in a different location. Cook an unfamiliar meal together. Choose something and commit to doing your best. It may not go as well as you'd like it to. It may be a disaster. Good—then you'll have an opportunity to practice your positive mindset while you build a memory to look back on and laugh.

CHAPTER 7

Improve Communication

Jason had been on the road for two weeks with various speaking gigs. When he got home that weekend, we'd taken Sunday to reconnect as a family and just to sit down to a couple of meals together. But Monday morning, it was back to work. First on the agenda was our quarterly meeting. Erica had pulled the reports together and we sat down in the conference room with our team.

Jay spoke first. "Morning, everyone. Thanks for all your support while I was gone. I've had a chance to look through things this morning, and I gotta tell you, priority one: Our marketing sucks right now. We definitely need to hire someone to run the website content and to manage the social media."

Jason was up and pacing, pointing to various reports. One of our staff members was taking notes, but Erica was frozen at the table, her face turning red. She finally spoke up.

"What do you mean, 'the social media'? What's wrong with it?" Erica had built the social media from scratch and continued running it in addition to sales, accounting, and everything else that didn't fall under someone else's job duties.

"Those numbers just aren't where we need them to be." Jay moved on to the next item in reports, not noticing that Erica was blinking back tears. She'd been here solo trying to manage everything while he'd been on the road, and then he blew in and ignored everything that she'd done.

She shoved down the anger and defensiveness and wondered if he was right. Maybe she wasn't doing as well juggling things as she needed to.

Jay was thirty minutes into the meeting before he finally noticed the tension in Erica's jaw and the red in her cheeks.

"Okay, let's pause for a second and take five," he said, trying to catch Erica's eye, but she fled the room before anyone else could even get to their feet.

"Shit," Jason said, sitting down at the table. "I gotta remember this isn't the SEAL teams."

Every Voice Matters

On a SEAL team, communication can literally mean the difference between life and death. In a SEAL platoon, there are roughly sixteen men led by a senior officer called the OIC, or officer in charge, an assistant platoon commander, a senior enlisted chief petty officer, and an LPO, or lead petty officer. Platoons are usually further divided into two squads: the OIC leading one with the LPO, and the enlisted chief petty officer leading the other with the assistant platoon commander. It's absolutely essential that these leaders are aligned. In a SEAL team with effective leadership, communication is one of the core skills that makes a leader stand out. The worst leaders are those who shut everyone else down the second they bring up a point. Their teammates quickly learn not to speak up at all, because it won't matter. When a team has a good leader who values each person's input, the entire team is stronger. On the SEAL teams, everybody has a voice. Even a new guy can bring something up he saw on the mission, and if it's a valid point, it's a valid point. His rank or tenure on the team doesn't matter.

When we do mission training and the after-action debriefing, whether it's a mission or a training, every single person in the room shares what they saw from their vantage point. Everyone listens because we know that we're in high-risk situations and no one person has all the intel by themselves. We need everyone's eyes and input to constructively evaluate the mission or training's success. You may not always like how someone describes your actions—you may even feel defensive about decisions you made—but in the end, we listen because communication makes us better. It helps us accomplish our missions, and it can even save our lives.

In a marriage, you both need to have an equal voice to work together as a team. If only one person is constantly making decisions, sharing feelings, and expressing issues then you're going to run into problems. Because the other person *does* have things to say—they are likely just bottling up that input to avoid conflict. Sooner or later that's going to backfire. So, how do you learn to have better conversations in both daily life and the difficult moments that can be challenging?

What Goes into Communication?

Most people believe they are strong communicators, but you only need to spend an evening eavesdropping on the couple at the table next to you at the restaurant to shatter that belief. Are they snarky to each other? Do they interrupt? Belittle or ignore the other when they're speaking? Our guess is all those things are happening more often than not, and especially in a marriage that's struggling. So, what's happening? Why do people think they are good at communication but then spend most of their time misunderstanding each other? Do we just need more active listening? Advanced comm classes? How can we start to hear each other, especially in marriage?

When you think of communication, most people think of talking, but that's only one small part of communication. It's far more complex.

At its most basic, communication includes verbal and nonverbal aspects. Essentially, you are expressing information every time you are in proximity to each other, whether in person, via text or email, or on the phone. All of those interactions reveal, and reflect, how you feel about your partner.

Verbal communication includes the words you're using, and some of us need to improve the way we use language to make sure we're not hurting each other unintentionally or making sure we get our message across clearly and in the best way.

Nonverbal communication is often louder and can overrule spoken words. If your spouse has ever rolled their eyes at you in the middle of a discussion, that nonverbal communication likely either escalated the discussion or shut down the conversation entirely as one of you left the room.

Another part of communication is listening. So often when people talk about listening, it's limited to active listening techniques where you repeat back what you think you've heard. There's nothing wrong with that; in the military we often repeat a command over the radio to affirm it, so that we're absolutely sure we understand. But in a military scenario, that repetition also results in coordinated action. Is your communication prompting coordinated action? If you want to move forward, to do things differently, you'll have to change how you talk and how you listen to each other. If that feels hard right now, remember the real goal of communication: to make your marriage stronger.

Let's say it again: **The goal of communication is to make your marriage stronger.** Every single time, every single interaction.

The goal is not to win. The goal is not to convince the person you're right. The goal is to make your marriage stronger. If you are listening to your partner with the goal of making your marriage stronger, you will.

How do you do that though? The method of communication, the way to actually make your marriage stronger, is to respectfully understand each other. Most people struggle to listen because they are more invested in their own message and keeping control of the moment. If you're only listening to respond or to counter your spouse, then you aren't really hearing them. If you're only listening to find holes in their argument, you might be missing the point entirely. If you're listening to your spouse explain a problem and you're formulating how to fix it while they are still talking, again, you aren't listening with the right goal in mind.

If you keep a stronger marriage as your central goal, it shifts everything else about the way you communicate. Suddenly, you aren't in a hurry to cut off your spouse, because that would express disrespect and harm your marriage over time. You're asking questions from a place of curiosity instead of judgment because you know how terrible it feels to be dismissed or judged while you're figuring something out, and you don't want your spouse to feel that way. You aren't blowing up when your spouse asks questions, because you're committed to working together instead of against each other.

Real communication in a marriage requires vulnerability, and you can't be a safe place to share information, feelings, and problems if you are not working together to get better. Part of why you might have trouble listening is because you don't trust each other—maybe you don't trust yourself. But it doesn't have to be that way. You can build a capacity for vulnerability and stronger communication.

Practice in Everyday Conversations

You can't learn how to be a stronger communicator in the middle of a heated argument. That skill must be developed in everyday conversations. You probably had quite a few of these while you were dating. But it's easy to forgo these conversations once you get married. If you've ever looked up at each other and tried to remember the last time you talked about something other than the house or the budget or the carpool, you know what we mean.

At minimum, you need to intentionally make time daily to check in with each other about things that have nothing to do with what we call "household management." If you've been out of the habit, it's going to be awkward. Go on a date (even if it's at your own table after the kids go to bed) and make a no talk of kids or work rule.

If you find you don't have anything to say, you've probably discovered a weak point in your lives and marriage. You're not roommates, dividing up bills and freezer space. If you've been so busy that your life is dominated by kids and work alone, maybe it's time to expand your conversations, interests, and life. Luckily, there are some shortcuts if you find you don't have much to say, such as apps and websites that have questions to discuss like the Gottman Card Decks, the Paired app, or the Agapé app. These games or apps have questions on a wide range of topics from simple questions like, "Would you like to be famous? Why or why not?" to personal and intimate questions like, "How would you like to keep sexual tension alive outside the bedroom?" You could even try that silly kids' game "Would You Rather." Anything to get you having everyday conversations that remind you that you are more than your work and your parenting (even when you love to talk about those things like we do!). It might feel awkward at first, but these outside resources can spark new directions in your conversations you may not have explored otherwise.

Once you've stopped staring blankly at each other, and you've begun to reestablish some daily communication, check-ins will start to feel more natural. You can both share what happened in your day, what was a challenge, what was fun, what you enjoyed.

If you have a habit of keeping everything bottled up inside, that's no good for you or your spouse. Start slow, but be consistent and you'll get into a healthy routine of discussing everything from your day to your hopes and dreams. This is how you build a culture of communication which will make tough conversations easier.

If you're the spouse who feels like they often have to bring up issues to be resolved in your marriage, put those on hold if you can during these daily conversations. Your partner can't hear you well if they think that every time you talk it's going to be about an issue.

Still, there are moments when real issues *do* need to be raised, and we'll talk more specifically about conflict in chapter 8. For now, though, let's look at how to avoid the communication busters that shut down connection along with the ways you can boost your conversation skills.

Communication Busters

Lots of things can shut down communication: disrespect, defensiveness, assumptions, and anger. All of them are rooted in insecurity, selfishness, or long-held patterns. If this sounds like the way you communicate, don't stand around arguing that this is just how you are. Bullshit. It might be that it is your first instinct, but if you value your spouse and marriage, you can make an effort to catch yourself when you pull one of these out. It won't be perfect every time, but the goal is progress. And if you notice that your spouse is trying to improve in these areas and making progress? Notice it. Appreciate it. And keep growing together, swapping out these busters for the communication boosters we'll discuss next.

Disrespect

Disrespect shuts down open communication. The Gottman Institute classifies disrespect as contempt, and they refer to it as one of the four horsemen that can doom a relationship. "Contempt comes from a place of superiority and makes the other feel inferior," they write. "Deep down, it stems from a sense of feeling unappreciated and unacknowledged in the relationship. It can take the form of verbal or non-verbal language, which can include sarcasm, mockery, and facial gestures." Marriages that allow contempt of any kind to bleed into interactions will not be able to effectively communicate because contempt communicates that you don't respect your partner. Notice that Gottman includes facial expressions here. If you feel contempt for your partner, you need to do some work to dig down and figure out where it began and root it out. No discussion can be productive if one of you is harboring contempt or disrespect. It would be worth asking each other, "Are there times when you feel I disrespect you?" Listen to each other's responses, and work to make sure both of you feel respected.

Defensiveness

Defensiveness can also hurt communication. It's that sting that makes you feel you must defend yourself. If you don't have much experience giving and receiving constructive feedback, everything will feel like a personal attack. Defensiveness can look like denial or combativeness, including turning on the person you're talking to in a negative way. Psychologist Dr. Seth Meyers explains that people often get defensive when they feel like they are losing control. If you find yourself easily defensive, take a minute before responding. Your body goes into overdrive as it tries to keep you safe. If you've never been able to receive feedback well, think about why that is. It can be a way to avoid dealing with your emotions, or to avoid accountability. The defensiveness is there to try to protect your ego, but it can come at a high cost. If you feel defensive in a conversation, take a beat and ask yourself what you're really trying to protect. Where is the defensiveness coming from? You have to learn to trust each other as partners, that anything you bring up in communication is there to make your marriage stronger—not to tear you down personally.

Assumptions

Assumptions run hand in hand with poor listening, but even when you've listened well you can jump to conclusions. Assumptions hurt communication because they imagine something more or something different than what it is being said, leading to misunderstandings and mistrust in some cases. For example, if your partner brings up your long work hours, don't assume they don't appreciate you or that they think you're having an affair or that they don't understand why you're working so hard. The antidote to assumptions is curiosity. The statement "Tell me more" genuinely can help you get to the bottom of what they truly mean. Some of us have imaginations or minds that work overtime creating problems where there might not be any. Our assumptions can actually do as much harm as the original issue if not handled well.

Anger

Anger and emotions aren't always the enemy. Plenty of couples get angry or overwhelmed with each other, but it's how they handle their anger during an argument and how they recover afterward that makes a difference in the health of the relationship. We are both passionate people, and we have definitely had angry discussions with each other. But we refuse to allow disrespect, name-calling, or other harmful tactics into our discussions whenever possible. As soon as one of us is too overwhelmed to continue the discussion, we might storm off, go for a drive, or retreat in tears. It doesn't mean the discussion is a failure, it means we have to cool off and come back to repair anything we've done or said while overwhelmed that didn't build up our marriage. We'll talk more about this in chapter 9. When we come back together, we usually begin with an apology on both sides. Don't let anger sabotage your communication regularly without making the necessary repairs afterward, learning from each discussion.

Communication Boosters

In turn, you can improve your communication pretty quickly by incorporating the following strategies in your daily lives together.

Full Respect

The flip side of contempt is full respect. Respect says: "We are both equal members of this team. We don't value one person's viewpoint over the other." This next piece of advice may feel uncomfortable depending on how you were raised, but it's important to make sure that one partner is not unilaterally making all or most of the decisions. We have never been in a place where one of us declared, "Look, this is just the way it's going to be. I've decided." Even if your intentions are in the right place, you're off course. Why? Your goal is to build a stronger marriage. It takes both of you. Think of it like lifting weights on leg day. If only one leg is getting a workout, only one leg is carrying the weight, the other leg atrophies and it will lead to alignment problems among other things. Full respect says we're figuring this out together because we both matter as equal partners here.

When we don't agree, we know the discussion isn't over yet. We do more research, write out pros and cons, think it over, or explore other options. It's important to note that we don't have to come to full agreement about a decision if we can reach a place where we understand each other and agree to try something. When Erica wanted to run the Bengal cat business, Jay was skeptical, and it took some convincing. As cool as the cats were, it wasn't his favorite idea. But Erica is his favorite *person*, so he agreed to support her as they began the business. Full respect. He trusted her to follow the business plan and communicate, and he did what he could to make sure it succeeded—building pens and helping, not harping over her shoulder anytime there was an extra expense or a roadblock.

Appreciation

Appreciation is one of the most overlooked ways to begin communicating better. The one rule: it must be honest and genuine. You can't bullshit your way through this one. Research shows that for every negative interaction between a couple, you need five positive moments to counter it. Those positive moments can begin with honest appreciation. Start noticing what your spouse is doing around the house, at work, with the kids—especially the ways they take care of things when no one is looking. Appreciation works on both the giver and the receiver. If you're giving appreciation, you are going to have a positive feeling when you realize your spouse is doing something for you and the marriage, and the receiver is going to be thankful you noticed. If contempt is a loop of doom, appreciation is a wheel of positivity that keeps generating more positivity. And appreciation doesn't have to cost anything but attention. It's hard to believe that something so quick and specific can have such long-lasting positive effects on your spouse, but it can. Get creative. Leave a note, send a text at an unexpected time, whisper something at bedtime without expecting anything in return except to build up your partner and your marriage. One tip: be specific. Saying, "Thanks for starting the coffee this morning, so it was ready when I got out of the shower" is much more specific than, "Thanks for your help this morning." Even if you're navigating a rocky period and you're both exhausted and a little irritated with each other, appreciation is a bridge that can begin to bring you back together as a team.

Perspective

Keep life's problems in perspective. After surviving life-threatening combat wounds and hundreds of hours in surgery and recovery, Jason laughs when someone at Starbucks goes on a rant about their order being wrong. How serious is this problem in the larger scope of things? Most things that we let ruin our days are more inconveniences (Jason calls them schedule disruptions in his talks and workshops) than true problems. Yes, those things can add up and really throw you for a loop in the moment, but use them as practice for the big things.

And when you're facing a true problem? Cancer, bankruptcy, a catastrophic loss? You're right. You're staring down the barrel of a gun on those, but it doesn't mean you have to turn on each other. Keeping perspective means looking at the long game, knowing that things right now might be tough, but you have what it takes to come through it as a couple. Perspective means acknowledging the tough battles you've already faced together, and knowing that you will make it through this one as well.

Letting Communication Work *for* You

That morning in the conference room during our quarterly meeting, Jason hadn't checked his directness. Erica made assumptions about what his words meant about the job she'd been doing. Erica was overwhelmed, and it kept us from having the conversation we needed to have. Luckily, we've built the skills to navigate these types of conversations many times over.

After a few minutes, Jay went in search of Erica.

"You ready to run?" he asked, deploying our inside joke from when we were dating, his face full of concern.

Erica wiped her eyes and shook her head, a small smile starting.

Jason came to meet her eye-to-eye. "I'm sorry—I realize the way I talked about the marketing and social media made you feel like shit, and we wouldn't have the numbers we have today without you."

"Sorry I froze," Erica said. "I've missed you the last couple weeks, and it's been a lot keeping everything afloat. What you said made me think maybe I wasn't doing as good a job as I thought. And it felt like you overlooked all we did to get to this point."

"You know me—I'm forward focused—ready for the next drive. So I appreciate you reminding me of how we got here. Do you feel like you're having to juggle too much? Would you even like someone else to come aboard to help with that stuff? I should have asked you before I blurted it out in front of everyone."

"I ... I don't know. Maybe we can look at what we're trying to do and make a more thought-out plan before we try to hire someone. I'm not sure it's the right time yet," Erica said.

"Okay," Jay said, reaching out a hand. "Let's put it on hold—maybe we can try to have some ideas and hard numbers by next month or quarter—I can help. Anything else before we go back?"

Erica's smile lit up her face. "Nope. We're good. No need to run, yet." And we both laughed.

INVINCIBLE MARRIAGE MOMENT

Communication requires both of you to contribute equally and with full respect. Build a foundation for stronger communication with everyday conversations, then work to listen and speak more effectively in tough situations.

REFLECT

1. Think about the meeting we had at the beginning of the chapter, and the way we resolved it at the end. Describe what each of us did to communicate.

2. Which of the communication busters are you currently pulling out too often? How can you plan ahead so you don't depend on it anymore?

FIRST STEP

Resolve to build in a communication booster each day. Start by finding something to appreciate in your spouse. Be genuine.

PART III

UNDER FIRE

This is what you've trained for. When adversity strikes, it's an opportunity to make your marriage stronger. Conflict and failure don't devastate an invincible marriage, they refine it. Learn the advanced skills you need to survive and thrive during life's greatest challenges.

CHAPTER 8

Face Conflict Together

Some of the most devastating losses in the military community occur in friendly fire incidents when warriors are killed by our own forces. It can be caused by miscommunication, cross fire, or even malfunctions in equipment that confuse the battlespace. When SEAL teams conduct close quarters combat training, we learn to assess and engage threats in an enclosed space where friendly fire is a constant risk. We have to learn to engage in combat without harming our own teammates.

For example, if we're entering a two-story building with one team upstairs and one on the bottom floor, instructors create scenarios that force us to come in contact with the other team in addition to the enemy at unexpected intervals. You can't be reactive and just shoot anyone in front of you with a gun. You have to learn how to assess potential threats very quickly.

That training became critical on the battlefield. In one firefight, our team was split as we pushed through some dense vegetation. It was extremely dangerous because enemy forces could be lying in wait between us. Any engagement might have us firing on our own guys. Within minutes, our leadership recognized the potential for friendly fire, and we communicated our intent to come back together. We were still separated by about a hundred yards when that firefight we anticipated actually did break out. The senior EOD (Explosive Ordnance Disposal) guy on the other team pulled his crew back to avoid a friendly fire catastrophe. Our training and communication saved lives, especially in conflict. We knew we couldn't avoid the conflict. We're warriors who are trained to run toward it. But we explicitly train to engage in a way that protected our teammates.

Conflict is where you see what you're made of. It is where military training goes to be tested, and it is where couples see how their foundation stands up under pressure. So much conflict goes unresolved because couples don't know how to fight on the same side with rules of engagement that allow you to fight without causing permanent damage. If you find yourself thinking of your spouse as the enemy, you've already lost. When we make our spouse the opponent during a fight, we're engaged in friendly fire, and we CANNOT WIN no matter what strategies we use.

So how do you face conflict as a team? What rules of engagement can you put in place to make sure you're not wounding each other when you're in conflict? Start by recognizing you are on the same team and enter conflict knowing that you want what is best for both of you, what is best for your marriage. It changes the way you engage. And no, that doesn't mean avoiding conflict.

You Can't Avoid Conflict

Some people try to avoid conflict at all costs. They would rather suffer in silence than have a hard conversation. The problem is that the conflict doesn't go away, and your partner isn't even aware it's building until there's an explosion.

Instead of avoiding conflict to keep the peace, think about how you can intervene early with clear communication. This doesn't mean nitpicking every little thing that irritates you. It means thinking about when an issue is serious enough that you need to address it, and making attempts to resolve it before it can get out of hand. Your approach here is everything.

Think back to the story we told in the introduction about Erica's intervention.

It was 2013, four years after Jason's life-threatening combat injury. Our nonprofit business was thriving, he was making a full recovery physically, and our family was healthy as we approached his retirement from the Navy and the release of his first book, *The Trident*. Everything should have been great. But Jason was dealing with the aftermath of so many years in combat and in recovery, his body trying to reach some kind of equilibrium. He thought he just needed more rest, a little more time, and he could fix everything himself. He withdrew, too tired to hang out with Erica or the kids. He knew he was going through the motions to get through the day, but he believed he didn't need help—he was the overcome guy—the never quit guy. He'd just charge through it and keep going.

But Erica felt the chasm growing wider between us. She'd tried to patiently nudge him toward time together. Encouraged him not to hole up and drink alone. Made every attempt to remind him how much she loved him, no matter what we were facing.

But it wasn't until that day we drove to Suffolk that she reached across and softly said, "This is how it starts, Jay. The beginning of the end of our marriage. We can't shut each other out."

She was calm. Clear. Her concern for him and for our marriage overshadowed everything else. And that got through to Jay. Of course, he felt defensive, but everything we had been through to that point, all the ways we had worked together to resolve issues early, it all paid off in that moment. Jay was able to truly hear her concern and realize he might need some help. Then he followed through and got the help he needed. Sure enough, there were some things happening physically that were impeding his ability to manage stress like he usually would, and one conversation and appointment led to another until he was able to get the specialized help he needed.

You might not need medical help. You might not need any kind of therapy, but you do need to be honest about what's happening daily in your marriage. When you intervene early and communicate without condemnation or blame, it creates the space for your partner to come alongside you to make changes.

The one thing that will help you intervene early like Erica is empathy. If you can try to see the situation through the eyes and feelings of your partner, it's much easier to talk about it without negativity or attacks. Combine empathy with some clear expectations of how you will handle conflict and you don't have to be afraid of conflict in your marriage anymore. So, let's look at how you can build your own rules of engagement to handle conflict better.

Rules of Engagement

In the military, we have clear rules of engagement that govern our actions, especially in conflict. Those rules define when, how, and to what degree we can use force. Our goal is always to use the minimum force necessary and reasonable for the situation. If you use deadly force when you could easily have restrained someone, you're going to face some serious consequences.

Your marriage needs those guardrails too. If you're going to learn how to fight better together, you need some rules of engagement that establish expectations. For us, in addition to remembering that we're on the same side, we have a few that we use to protect our marriage, even when we're in the middle of a fight.

1. No ultimatums
2. No name-calling
3. No digs at the past

These three things are off limits for us, as they are no different than shooting a teammate in a friendly fire incident. Here's why:

No Ultimatums

An ultimatum is a demand designed to shut down a discussion or end a negotiation. In effect, it says, "Do this or I'm out." An ultimatum doesn't show respect for your partner because it doesn't leave room for compromise. From the earliest days in our relationship, we committed not to throw around the word divorce because it felt like an ultimatum. For some couples, divorce might be the right choice when they've exhausted all other avenues. But for us, we love each other and are actively seeking the best for each other, so we aren't going to issue the ultimatum of divorce (or any other ultimatum) in conflict.

No Name-calling

When we fight, we absolutely refuse to call each other names or to fling negative personal attacks at each other. Name-calling is unproductive and hurtful at the very least, but it can also easily slip into verbal abuse. Even once you resolve a conflict, those hurtful names or personal attacks will live on in your partner's mind, often on repeat. Name-calling is like shooting a bullet at your partner—they might survive it, but it's going to leave a mark. Don't do it.

No Digs at the Past

In the middle of conflict, it can be difficult to stay in the moment, to make sure you're actually talking about the current issue. When we fight, we don't allow ourselves to reach back to old mistakes or situations that have been resolved. If you have fights that devolve into words like "You always . . ." or "You never . . ." you are likely reaching for the past. If you need to deal with a past hurt or you're in the middle of an ongoing conflict, try not to roll out a set of receipts that only shows you're keeping score. Allow each other to apologize, to try to do better, and when you fight, deal with the problem you're experiencing right now.

YOU CAN BORROW our rules of engagement or create your own, but clear expectations will go a long way in helping you work through conflict when it arises. You're on the same team, so love and care for each other enough to create these boundaries that will keep you both safe and your marriage protected no matter how fierce your disagreement. Once you know what's off limits in a fight, you can work through conflict in productive ways.

STOP Conflict in Its Tracks

When there's internal conflict in a SEAL team, good leadership pulls everyone together and hashes it out. Nothing is off the table, and guys can voice things that are going wrong, their opinions on decisions, or personality conflicts as long as we keep the good of the team in sight. Once that conversation is done, the facts are reviewed and decisions are made, and it's over. It doesn't mean you always agree with the outcome or get what you want, but you've had space to voice your frustrations and share your view. The goal of these sessions is always to build the team up—it's never to isolate or tear an individual down.

With practice, you can do the same in your marriage. Start by knowing and loving all aspects of your spouse. You don't have to agree on everything (and often won't!), but loving them means believing the best about them and working with them for your mutual benefit.

Once you're firmly grounded in that love for your spouse, STOP and make sure you take the time to communicate well for better conflict resolution every time.

Here's how you STOP conflict in its tracks:

S—Specific
T—Track understanding
O—Ownership and repair
P—Plan and take action together

Specific

When you are communicating in the midst of conflict, most people fall into generalizations or past mistakes instead of being specific about the immediate problem. When you generalize, you make blanket statements that don't necessarily apply to this specific situation: "You always pick fights with my mother!" or "You never help with chores!" Generalizations won't help you get to the root of the problem or find a solution, and they often turn into attacking someone's character. Instead, **be specific.**

What problem are you experiencing today? How are you feeling about it? How does it affect you? What is your request about how your partner can address it, if anything, and when should they address it?

If the problem today is about a fight with an extended family member, be specific. For example: "I noticed you arguing with my mom, and then she sent me a bunch of texts. I don't like feeling like I'm the go-between. I'm on your side. How can I help you feel more supported?"

Notice how this dialogue is focused on this instance. It describes the specific actions they noticed. They use "I" statements to clearly explain what they are feeling. And they invite further discussion. This is exactly how SEAL teams debrief, hearing each person's specific perspective.

Track Understanding

If you are listening to your spouse outline a specific problem, listen!

Listening does not mean agreeing. Listening means you fully take in your partner's concerns. If you don't understand a part of it, ask questions. Your tone and attitude are paramount here. Make your best attempt to see the problem from their perspective, again, even if you don't see it the same way. It can sound like active listening—"What I hear you saying is . . ."—but it can also just sound like clear, kind empathy: "I can see why that's so upsetting." Make sure you take a beat to acknowledge what your spouse has said before jumping in to react.

Ownership

Here is where most conflict conversations go wrong. No one takes ownership or attempts to repair the damage, no matter the magnitude. Once you've heard the problem, once you are sure you understand what is happening from your spouse's point of view, take ownership of your part of the problem. Apologize if needed. In a conflict conversation, it's easy to get defensive and want to turn attention to your spouse and their part. Don't start there—start with you.

The most elite SEAL operators in the world sometimes make mistakes, even when they're trained to the highest standards.

When that happens, those warriors own the error, address corrections or next steps, and move forward, stronger for the experience. When Jason was a mobility force commander on the ground in Iraq, part of his job was checking the codes that were necessary for communication between different forces we'd encounter on the ground. It was a safeguard to ensure the team knew who was in the vicinity. One night, he'd missed checking the codes, and when they came across a Marine unit, he didn't have the right codes to confirm they were friendly forces. It could have cost them lives. Later during the debrief, Jason felt defensive at first—the codes hadn't changed in a month—but then he recognized that he needed to admit the error and explain what had happened to ensure it didn't happen again. He went to leadership and owned it, winning their respect and preserving his ability to lead well.

What might ownership sound like in our example between a spouse and mother? "I'm sorry my mom was on you. I probably haven't noticed her doing that or how it's affected you in the past." Notice how in this case, they weren't even involved in the negative interaction, but they still took ownership of what they hadn't noticed—both about the interactions and the way they affect the spouse. Be genuine in this step. Own what you can and don't be afraid to apologize.

Plan

While these steps don't have to be done sequentially, eventually you'll want your communication to evolve into action. Hopefully ownership softens both people and allows you to start figuring out how to move forward together. Some problems may just need airing and awareness brought to them, so that the next time it happens, you can act differently. Some need time and attention, maybe a reprioritization of time or resources.

In our example, this might sound like: "I probably haven't noticed her doing that or how it's affected you in the past. I can have a conversation with her if you want and ask her to respect your wishes or we can set a different boundary with her. What other ideas do you have?"

Whatever it takes, work together until you come to a solution that resolves the issue as best as you can with the information and resources you have right now. It doesn't have to be perfect to make progress.

When you STOP to communicate clearly, you avoid misunderstandings, hurt feelings, and damaging attacks you can't take back. Some problems will take more than one conversation. Maybe the problem requires some research, some outside help, or some space. Commit to working through it together. If you notice a problem keeps coming up, start looking at how it's matching up with your core values as a couple. It may be that your beliefs are significantly different on the problem, and you need a compromise you can both agree on. Choose to let disagreements make you stronger as a couple.

Learning from Conflict = Invincible Team

Conflict is where you learn what you've truly built. You're going to have some knock-down-drag-outs you regret—we make mistakes. Just like the friendly fire in close quarters combat training, conflict is a place to evaluate where you have built trust and where you are still vulnerable. If you take the time to work together through those vulnerabilities, you'll come back stronger and better able to withstand the pressure of conflict.

INVINCIBLE MARRIAGE MOMENT

Your spouse is not the enemy. You can't avoid conflict, but you can learn to manage it in a way that makes your team stronger by being specific, tracking understanding, taking ownership, and making a plan. Conflict can reveal weak points, but that also means it is a place where you can work together to learn and grow.

REFLECT

1. Does conflict in your marriage feel like friendly fire that ultimately harms you both? Or like you're a team facing the same problem together?
2. What are your rules of engagement? Discuss together.
3. Look back at the section on how to STOP conflict in its tracks. Which step do you need the most work implementing?

FIRST STEP

Choose a time you can sit down together to think about your last argument, no matter how it ended. Apply the STOP steps and talk through what you could have said during the fight. Be specific about how it feels different to make sure you're working together on a solution.

CHAPTER 9

Know When to Give Space

Jason told the story of our courtship in his first book, *The Trident*, but now we'd like to tell that same story from Erica's perspective.

As we wrote in chapter 1, Jay and I met in a bar in Louisville, Kentucky. We had an instant connection, and I could tell there was something different about him. We talked long into the night, and I invited him to a barbecue the next day, knowing full well my young son would be there. You can tell a lot about a man by how he reacts to a woman when he finds out she has a baby. Up until Jason, there hadn't been anyone who embraced my son fully, and that was nonnegotiable for me in a partner. When Jay arrived, I could tell he was surprised, but he jumped in, playing with Austin and getting along great with my friends. It was a terrific afternoon all around, and I felt hope that maybe this was someone who could go the distance with us, someone whom I could build a life with.

Any time Jason had time off from training, he would drive over from Fort Knox to be with us. We had so much in common, and genuinely had a blast together. A month later, I invited him to meet my family on Easter Sunday. He came. Again, Jason passed the family test with flying colors. He was personable and fun. My grandmother, G.G., loved him.

But I still thought he was a boxer. Finally, near the end of our second month dating, Jason sat me down and told me the truth about his work—that he was a Navy SEAL stationed in Virginia Beach, and that it would impact our relationship sooner or later. He was worried. He outlined how hard military life was for spouses and families; he made no promises that he'd always be home or that he wouldn't be in danger. It was a life that often required moves and upheaval, and he wanted me to be sure I could see myself being a part of that lifestyle. I listened, weighing his concern with my own mixed feelings. My family and support system was all here in Kentucky. Could I really leave that behind when I had a young son to consider too? I decided Jay was worth the risk. We made plans as he finished his last training cycle in Kentucky: Austin and I would visit him in Virginia in a few weeks.

Jay left for Virginia Beach, and we began a long-distance relationship. We sent long emails to each other and connected through calls. It was hard to be apart. Here I'd found someone who made my life feel complete, and he was hundreds of miles away. Our emails and calls only cemented the feeling that we needed to be together. We dreamed about travel and diving and adventures together. When Austin's doctors recommended surgery to check the pressure on a hole in his heart and determine whether additional surgery might be needed, Jason listened to my fears about my young son having surgery. When I scheduled it close to Christmas, Jay promised to come and hold me while Austin was under the knife. I was no longer facing life's highs and lows alone.

By November, it felt like just a matter of time before we'd make something more permanent. I already wanted to be with him every minute of every day—the physical separation was painful. At Thanksgiving, Jason invited me and Austin, then only fifteen months old, to meet his family in North Carolina. His mom, sister, and I clicked right away, and the weekend felt like a dream.

So nothing could have surprised me more than when we hit the road at the end of the weekend to head back to Virginia Beach. Jay was driving and his body was full of tension. Something was wrong. My mind combed over the weekend again. Was it something I had said? What happened?

Finally, I just asked outright. "What's wrong?"

His response was a short, sullen, "Nothing."

We rode in silence for a while, until I couldn't stand it anymore. I asked again. "Jay, what is it? What happened? What's wrong?"

This time, he exploded. I knew he had a short fuse. We'd talked about it, but this time the flurry of words that came pouring out were directed at me.

"We shouldn't be together. This is never going to work. My job is too much. We hate being long-distance now? Ha! My job is going to separate us over and over again. It's not worth the heartache."

I listened carefully for anything that we hadn't already considered, but I was unconvinced. "Jason, we can make it work. I'm not worried."

"You should be worried! Besides, it would never work. I like things structured, ordered, and you . . . you don't care about that. You let things slide around the house, you prefer spontaneity, and I can't live that way. You want things I can't give."

Now he was getting closer to an issue I knew we'd have to compromise on if we got married. Of course I knew he was regimented, structured, a neat freak. And while I didn't let things get dirty, I tended to be more of a free spirit, knowing the housework would still be there after the fun. Hearing the finality in his voice, I broached a question.

"What does this mean?" I asked.

"It means we're through."

His words sliced through me. I could tell he meant them. He didn't offer any other option. There was no apology, no argument, no negotiation held out for me to grasp. I sat in silence the final hour of our trip back to Virginia Beach trying to understand what was happening. When we arrived, I transferred Austin's car seat back into my own car and quickly packed our things, fighting angry tears. It was after midnight when I finally pulled out of the drive, Jay on the porch watching. No hug goodbye. No offers to call. Nothing.

I was furious.

It took over ten hours to drive from Virginia Beach to Louisville, Kentucky, and I spent most of it replaying our relationship in my head. Had I missed signs? We'd been together for eight months. Eight months. I'd been so sure he would stick. We were in near constant contact, and now that was just gone? Because of his job and my free spirit? What the hell?

I held out hope that the next day maybe he would call or email, even if only to ask if we made it okay. No call came. No email. Not that day or for two weeks after. Fine, I thought. He's shown me something about who he is. I need to believe him.

I couldn't wallow. I had to work. I had to care for my son. I had Austin's surgery coming up, and we had Christmas to consider. I knew it would be tough. We needed a party, and I scheduled it for the night before Austin's surgery—hoping it would help keep my mind off of things. I got to work.

A couple weeks into December, that call from Jason I would have likely picked up the morning I arrived back in Louisville finally came. I didn't pick up. There was nothing to say. Jason's words and actions, and then his silence in the weeks since, had communicated where we stood loud and clear. I ignored the calls for a few days. When they didn't slow down, I answered and told him to drop dead.

It didn't deter him. He left messages. I didn't respond.

The night before Austin's surgery, the house was decorated, the food and drinks set out in the kitchen, and I was looking forward to all the friends coming over for our Christmas party.

The doorbell rang. It was still a little early, but everything was ready. I smoothed down my top before answering the door, grateful that I would be surrounded by friends that night instead of sitting alone with my son worrying about his procedure. I pulled open the door and frowned. It was Jay. He looked like a wild man, disheveled but hopeful.

"Hi," he said.

I set my jaw, trying to ignore how much I missed him—how seeing him brought all those months back to my chest and made it hard to breathe. "Hi."

He stood there not speaking. He finally shook himself and sputtered alive. "I told you I'd be here for Austin's surgery tomorrow, and I keep my word. I know I screwed this up—I got scared. I'm so sorry, Erica. I love you so much—you're it for me. I'm here to beg for your forgiveness. If there's any chance . . . I drove through freezing temperatures and a snowstorm with no back window in my Jeep.* I almost died in an accident, I just couldn't stay away."

I let him come inside, not fully trusting yet. But it was a first step. The space had clarified what he wanted, and then he had changed his actions to begin to win me back.

What We Do Instead of Healthy Space

Whether you're having a freakout like Jay or a meltdown in the midst of a vicious conflict, space might be the last thing you

---

* Apparently Jay's dog ate it—poetic justice.

consider. When your body is on high alert in an argument, when you're feeling attacked, so many of the decision-making parts of your brain shut down trying to keep you safe. If you freeze during a fight? That's your brain trying to keep you safe. If you flee during a conflict? That's your brain seeking safety. If you find yourself spewing things at your partner you would never say under normal circumstances, that's your fight response. These stress responses are hardwired deep in our biology—but they don't always serve us well in relationships.

The exact variety of a person's stress response can often be traced back to what they saw growing up or their early relationship experiences. Sometimes a fight response comes out as passive-aggressiveness. Sometimes a freeze response looks like stonewalling and refusing to engage. Sometimes a fight response looks like a flood of demands to stay and work through the problem when maybe your partner isn't ready.

Sometimes, if you're conflict averse, you're willing to drop or ignore the problem in favor of keeping the peace, but that doesn't work long-term. Early on, Erica's tears caused Jason to keep applying pressure, to solve things and make her happy again. But it doesn't work that way—pressuring when someone needs space makes it worse. It's like throwing fuel on a fire. It's especially hard to stop yourself because reducing your partner's distress would make you feel better too.

Jason sought space to try to protect himself from commitment, and the misconceptions he held about how it would change him. In one night, he tore down all we'd built over the better part of a year. His actions broke trust. Erica responded by creating her own space: respecting his decision even though she thought it was bullshit, and protecting herself and her son by not answering his calls. The space she enforced gave him the room he needed to imagine a life without her, and he was absolutely miserable.

What Is Space?

We often hear the phrase "taking space" in a relationship and instantly think of a breakup. Sometimes that's accurate. When Jay broke up with Erica out of fear, he took space, and Erica enforced that space. Jay learned that sometimes space and quiet speak louder than words. Erica was incredibly hurt by Jason's actions. She'd spent nearly a year thinking this might be the one guy that could go the distance with her and her young son. We'd met each other's families. To throw that away felt like a rash betrayal, and Erica knew that she couldn't pursue it further without some pretty drastic action that could counter the loss she felt. She didn't want to always wonder if he was going to cut away his parachute on our relationship early.

There was also the space created early in our relationship by our distance apart, with Erica in Kentucky and Jason in Virginia Beach. That space forced us to make time for each other through communication via email, the phone, and driving to each other when we could make it work. Long-distance relationships can get old fast if they aren't grounded in something more than physical chemistry, but that's also why physical distance can clarify a relationship. That long-distance space started a foundation we continue to build on today.

So space can be either positive or negative, all depending on how it's used. Marriage is about learning how to navigate its push and pull. Sometimes you absolutely need to walk away from an issue with your spouse to keep it from escalating. Sometimes you might need time to understand an issue or build some coping skills or ask better questions.

When you think of space, it's probably wise to shoot for the least amount needed. Space can't replace problem-solving and conflict resolution, the same way that Jay couldn't just call Erica and say "we're good" after breaking up with her. It took time to rebuild that trust and set a course together. So, if it is a minor issue that you're both heated about, the space you need might be a couple hours or overnight. We know a lot of people say not to let the sun go down on your anger, and while we've committed to it, the truth is that sometimes you need a little longer to cool off and see the thing more objectively. There's no sense revisiting an issue if you aren't both able to come to it clear-headed with your relationship as the main focus instead of your own individual hurt.

There may be times you need more space. Some couples have incorporated space as a part of a larger plan to refocus themselves and come to the marriage better. But space can't be productive if the time apart is spent pursuing affairs or binge drinking or other unhealthy behaviors. You can't make your marriage strong if you don't lead yourself well.

When Space Is Needed

Anytime a partner is too tired, emotional, or irrational, you need to take a minute. When Erica is overwhelmed with a problem at work, Jason understands he can't keep pushing. He has to take his foot off the gas and let her take a break for an hour or two at least. Luckily, we've learned over time with practice how to recognize when a break is needed sooner, but awareness is the first step.

Awareness runs in two directions. First, you need to be aware of yourself and the energy or attitude you're bringing to the situation. If you're amped up, angry, growling, it isn't a good time to launch into a heart-to-heart, no matter how much you want to sort through the thing right now. Likewise, if you are completely shutting down emotionally, unable to truly hear what your partner is saying, it's time to call a time-out. Know your own state. If you pay attention to your body, you can probably tell right away what's happening, whether it's tensing up, your voice pitching higher or faster, or your breathing becoming erratic. There are real physiological things that happen to your body in conflict, so pay attention. In military training, we talk about how to manage fear. Fear is a natural response to the unknown. It requires courage to face it, but you can also manage the stress of fear by knowing you've prepared for the battle, you've checked your gear, you've completed training. You can slow your breathing and focus on the task at hand. If you are in a place where you can't manage that fear, you may need to take a beat before responding.

The other way you need to harness awareness is in paying attention to your partner. If you notice that they are short in their responses, nonresponsive, defensive, or angry, you might need to ask if you can take a break and come back to the issue later. Sometimes it will be a matter of hours, other times it might be a few days.

We run our business together, and there have been many times we don't see eye-to-eye on something. Most of the time we can work it out, but when we're under a lot of pressure or Jay's been traveling, we're more likely to run into problems.

Say Jay is off on the speaking circuit, kicking ass, networking, and getting his talks done. Meanwhile, Erica and the team are back in Virginia running socials, contact outreach, membership services, logistics, contracts, retail operations, and event-booking. Both of us are tired and stressed during those high-tempo seasons because we're being stretched. So, if Jay comes back from a week away and sees a problem, his nature is to jump in and try to solve it directly as quickly as possible. At times, he forgets that Erica or another on their team may be aware of the problem and already working toward a solution. If he begins asking rapid-fire questions, sometimes that comes off as insensitive or aggressive.

If Erica's exhausted from running everything at home and work, those questions sometimes make her feel like he thinks she sat around while he was gone, when she definitely didn't.

Early in our business years, that would have snowballed into a huge fight. Today, we know when to ask for space, and how to do it so that our partner knows we aren't avoiding a problem—we just need a minute.

Maybe for your marriage it's stuff around the house. If one of you comes home from work, and the house feels like chaos, it's easy to imagine that your spouse didn't do anything all day. Even if you don't say anything directly, rage cleaning the moment you come in the door can send just as clear of a judgmental message.

Instead of reacting in the moment, ask about your spouse's day; what was tough and how you can help. No one wants to feel attacked the moment they come in the door—not you and not your spouse.

Ironically, sometimes just giving each other a minute to unwind makes you take a step back to think about what you're bringing into the situation. So many times in our marriage, Erica will come back after a break and say, "Sorry, I was overly emotional. Let's try again." Jay will come back and say, "Sorry I didn't consider your feelings, I was too direct. I needed to handle that differently."

That lays the groundwork to productively address the problem at hand. Now we recognize each other's triggers and if we accidentally set them off, we know to give a little bit of space and then come back to fix it.

How to Give Space

Clearly, we were both well-versed in giving space by walking away—not always the most productive tool if you want to stay in a relationship. Consider how you usually handle the heat of the moment. Is your first instinct to pull back? To leave? To go silent? Or are you more hotheaded and likely to go into full-court press defensive mode, getting loud and agitated? Spend some time thinking about prior relationships, and especially how you saw space being given in the home where you grew up. Maybe your parents never fought in front of you, so you have no idea what to do when things get tense. It can be especially difficult if you're the only one in your marriage reading this book and trying to do something different. But the good news is this: you can begin to change, even if your partner isn't fully on board yet. In fact, learning to give space might open up new opportunities to connect with your partner that weren't even possible in your old patterns. Let's look at how to effectively give space.

Timing

Timing is critical. In the heat of the moment, it can be hard to slow down and ask for space. It's much better to know ahead of time how each of you prefers to signal that you need space. It can be as simple as saying, "I want to hear you, but I need to call a time-out." If your partner continues to push, take a broken record approach and repeat: "I need to take a minute, please."

It's best if you can agree on a time to reconvene—whether an hour or a day later. You can also ask for a check-in before the discussion ensues. A simple "How are you feeling, is this a good time to talk about it?" can go a long way to helping both of you feel ready. Your first goal is to just begin noticing when you need space and to take it.

Pay attention to your and your partner's natural rhythms and personal preferences. If your spouse isn't a morning person, don't meet them at the coffee maker with a list of requests—that's a recipe for disaster. If you know your partner goes to bed early, planning a discussion right before bed is just setting you up for failure before you begin. Be mindful of when your partner is better able to engage the issue fully.

We also know that there isn't always going to be an ideal time. Compromise and set a timer if you have to, and do the best you can with the time you have set aside. Don't wait so long after the initial ask to discuss. If you say you'll try again in an hour, then do it. Trust is built when you follow through with action consistently. When Jay showed up at Erica's door that December, he was hoping his actions could begin a conversation that she wouldn't have with him over the phone. It took time, but it worked.

It's not going to be easy. It's going to take some trial and error, but stick with it and over time, we bet you'll find you are able to work through issues more quickly and with fewer angry exchanges. But the end goal is to grow closer and to better understand each other. To take care of your team and show you care. You can't do that if you're flooding them with emotional outbursts and heated discussions. Full mutual respect takes two people who want the best for each other, and sometimes taking space is what is needed. Jay needed space to figure out what he wanted while we were dating. And while he may not have taken it in the most respectful way, that space clarified how much he wanted our relationship in a way almost nothing else could have.

Reengage After Space

You have to reengage after you've taken the time-out. Every time. Resist the urge to brush things under the rug and to pretend that it didn't matter. If you said things you regret before you took some space, start with an apology and own your behavior. If you haven't done this before, it is going to feel uncomfortable. Do it anyway. Losing a marriage is far worse. Use "I" statements (like "I'm sorry I yelled over you" or "I'm sorry I assumed you didn't care about us") and resist the urge to blame or focus on your partner's behavior as you get started. Use the STOP method from the last chapter to engage conflict if needed.

If you're a partner who loves to go into fix-it mode, like Jason, you need to slow down and listen first. Don't assume that you've solved everything in your time apart and all you need to do is present your three-point fix-it plan and all will be well. Your plan might be great, but part of what caused the need for space was that one or both of you likely didn't feel heard and that caused things to escalate.

Once you've apologized, start by outlining the problem. Keep your statements short and focused on facts as much as possible. If feelings or opinions are involved—and they usually are!—make sure you're only stating your view as one possible view. Leave room for both of you to see an issue differently. We can't tell you how many times we've disagreed about something, but when we finally calmed down we saw the problem and solutions clearly but from different perspectives because of our experiences and history. And that isn't bad. Release your need to be right, and instead think more about how to hear what your partner is saying and how you can at least try to see their perspective, even if you disagree.

Not all problems can be solved with just one conversation. When Jason finally drove to Louisville to win Erica back, it took showing up in multiple ways to regain the trust that had been lost. He owned his fear, that he had bolted because he was afraid of commitment and knew it would take time to regain Erica's trust. Jay stayed in Louisville with Erica and Austin for three weeks, showing her that he was serious. That she was what he wanted.

Together, we talked about what commitment would look like in our relationship, and we both followed through on those promises.

The Result: Invincible Team

When you get better at reading each other, knowing when your partner is escalating, you can even gently offer space before something explodes either between you or with someone else. Erica can tell when Jason is getting wound up. His voice gets louder, and she knows when his body language reflects a situation about to get out of hand. She often suggests they leave the area or she'll change the subject, heading off an explosion or confrontation with someone else. Sometimes it is as simple as disrupting the flow with a request for a glass of water or trading plates. At that point, it's enough of a signal that Jason usually realizes what's happened and he can de-escalate the rest of the way himself. But together, we make each other better. We keep each other in check subtly, and it builds trust over time.

Once you get used to giving and taking space, you'll also realize that you are both stronger when you support each other individually. You don't have to comment on every venture your partner takes or argue when they want to try a course of action, no matter how much you think it's not going to work. If they ask your opinion, offer it respectfully, but let each other make choices and mistakes, confident that your marriage can stay strong and withstand it.

After Jay's combat injuries, he drove hard through recovery, determined to get back on the battlefield. He talked about it week in and week out. It motivated him from the first day in Bethesda. His identity was so tightly aligned with his SEAL brotherhood that not joining them again was inconceivable. At any point, Erica could have said, "That's not going to happen—it's just not realistic." She certainly thought it. But instead, she chose to trust that he would recover, and time would tell what he would be able to do as a SEAL. She trusted him to know his limits when we came to that decision, and that we would be able to face the next chapter whatever came. Space doesn't have to destroy a marriage. Use it strategically and you'll find yourself stronger than you thought possible.

INVINCIBLE MARRIAGE MOMENT

Space can be strategically used in your marriage to respect each other's needs. Create a process for how you communicate the need for space and how you'll reengage to make sure neither of you feels neglected or unheard.

REFLECT

1. Have you had a positive or negative experience when given space in the past?
2. What does it feel like when you are overwhelmed and need space?
3. How do you currently take space in healthy or unhealthy ways?

FIRST STEP

Discuss a time when you needed space and either did or didn't receive it. If it's too difficult to use an example from your marriage, consider using an example from your past or outside life. Listen with empathy to each other. Then identify how you'd like to signal when you need space in a tense situation or argument. Create that phrase that will let your partner know you just need a minute to regroup. Then use it the next time you feel overwhelmed or need space.

CHAPTER 10

Turn to Humor

Jason was in SEAL training at BUD/S, and they had just finished Hell Week. His team was in hydro-reconnaissance training, a series of exercises to teach them how to use a combination of boat skills, swimming, and diving to gather intel near a beach target. They don't even do this training anymore because technology can map out the bottom of beaches now, but back then, it was still a core part of training. They'd go out on the water and use ropes with weights and a slate to make notes underwater to chart the bottom of the beach in preparation for an amphibious landing using explosives or a breach or whatever the mission required.

Hell Week is aptly named. Getting through it wrecks your mind and body, and you're willing to do almost anything to help your body survive it. So, when we heard we were going out into the water to do the hydro-recon exercise, a bunch of us tried to cheat by wearing an additional layer of wetsuit under the crappy wetsuit we'd been issued in training. It's probably evidence that our brains weren't fully functioning after Hell Week to think that we'd get it past the instructors, but either brazen defiance, optimism, or stupidity had us all lined up wearing cheater tops under our wetsuits.

An inspection ensued before the exercise began and sure enough, twenty-five of us were busted with the additional wetsuit layers.

"Strip!" the order came. Not only were we not going to have an extra layer, but now we had to do the exercise in just our PT shorts without a wetsuit. When the hydro-recon exercise was over that morning, everyone was dismissed except for the twenty-five of us who had tried to cheat. The instructors put us through a bunch of obstacles and exercises as punishment for trying to get around them.

At one point, as we stood shivering, trying to regain our strength, one of the instructors addressed the senior man of the group, Ensign Gus Kaminski, who was shivering right along with the rest of us.

"Mr. Kaminski," the instructor barked. "We're running out of things to make you do. We need you to think of something creative to finish off this punishment. It's going to continue until somebody quits."

We stared at Gus, willing him to choose something that would let us off a little easier. None of us was going to quit—not after making it through Hell Week.

"Well, sir," Kaminski said, "we got in trouble for trying to cheat the cold, so you should probably punish us with the cold from the surf."

Groans rose up around the group.

"Son of a bitch," we muttered. Others cursed him for being the senior man.

"Yes! Surf torture," the instructor shouted. "Go!"

We marched down to the water and lay on our backs in the cold surf, feet pointed toward the shore, Kaminski right in the middle of us all. We locked arms and sputtered through each wave that crashed over our heads in the frigid March Pacific surf. Freezing temps, salt, sand, water up our noses, down our throats, in every crevice that hadn't already gone numb.

The first few waves, there were jokes and general cursing, but thirty minutes in, we suffered in silence, the only sound the roar of the surf, the chattering of our teeth, the sputtering of each man down the line desperate to suck in enough air to stay conscious between waves, and the occasional shout from instructors encouraging us to all quit.

It's a mental game. Stay focused. Don't let your mind give in. Force your body to comply. Stick together. Over and over and over, praying for the end.

After a particularly large wave passed, Kaminski raised his head a little and mustered enough voice to shout down the line, "Hey guys?"

"What?" we angrily answered.

"You know, when they asked me about the whole cheat the cold thing and I said we should, you know, be punished by the cold?"

A chorus mixed with "Yes" and "Son of a bitch" rose from the surf torture line in reply.

Gus waited a moment and said, "That was a really bad idea."

Another wave crashed and every man in line came up from it laughing his head off.

"Get out!" the instructors on the beach yelled.

Within minutes, the instructors released us, and we trudged back up the beach to try to get warm, each of us still muttering and chuckling between chattering teeth.

We were confused. If the instructors said an exercise would continue until someone quit, the exercise continued until someone quit. They didn't play about directives like that. But that morning, our ability to stick together, to laugh and find a way through the misery together must have struck a chord with them.

Jason didn't realize until much later how that kind of shared humor in the midst of misery was a necessity. On dangerous missions in Iraq and Afghanistan, there was often a lot of chatter on the radio, people cracking jokes, trying to lighten what could have been a very dark mood.

Marriage can benefit from humor in the same way, but it can be a minefield if you don't think carefully about how and when to use it. Remember that your goal is always to strengthen the relationship—to make your team stronger. When you keep your spouse's feelings in mind, and pay attention to the moment, humor can be one of the most cathartic things you can use to defuse a difficult situation or help lighten the mood when things are serious.

Why Humor?

No matter how hard things are in the moment, humor can make it more bearable. Here are just a few reasons to make humor a priority as you work to strengthen your marriage.

Bonding

If you've ever had an inside joke with someone, then you understand what we mean when we say that humor bonds people together. It's not just a feeling either. A 2017 study published by researchers at the University of North Carolina, Chapel Hill, found that when two people shared laughter it made them feel like they shared similarities and made them want to spend more time together. Just like Jason and his team in the surf exercise, humor tightened bonds that might otherwise have been tested.

Maybe you feel like you don't have many or any shared humorous moments in your marriage now, but it doesn't mean you can't build them. What creates an inside joke? An experience you share where humor erupts, either on purpose or without planning.

When you say, "Remember that time . . ." and share it again (hopefully to laughter), bam. Inside joke. Shared humor and fun make you feel closer to someone.

Relief

When done well, humor provides much-needed relief. That relief gives enough breathing room to stand back and reevaluate the situation. It makes it easier to keep going. When our SEAL team was half-drowned in the surf that day after hydro-recon training, Kaminski's joke gave enough relief that we could have kept going, had the instructors not pulled us immediately from the water. It helped us manage the very real physical and mental stress we were under.

Humor likely won't *solve* whatever problem you're facing as a couple, but it can make it easier to shoulder together. But you have to learn to read your spouse and the situation to know when it's the right time, and not overuse jokes when you're in the middle of a serious situation.

Perspective

The final reason to use humor in your marriage is that it reminds you both of the big picture. As we write this book, we're in the middle of a new business venture, including a new building. It's been challenging to say the least. When we're in tense discussions, trying to work through the logistics and near-constant decision fatigue, one of us will often break the tension with, "Let's buy a building! It will be so great!" And we both laugh. It reminds us that what we're facing is temporary, while our relationship has gone the distance. Let humor give some much-needed perspective on what's happening. Again, it won't solve the problem, but it might be enough to put the problem in its proper context, so it doesn't feel so overwhelming.

But what if you feel like you aren't funny? Do you just need to go learn a few jokes? How do you develop a sense of humor?

Humor Theories

Writer E. B. White famously cautioned against trying to over-think humor. "Explaining a joke is like dissecting a frog. You understand it better but the frog dies in the process." But you don't have to become a comedian to understand how humor works and to think about how to use it (and not use it) in your relationships. You just have to pay attention. That said, a couple theories might help, especially if you want to avoid humor that hurts.

Superiority

Early philosophers like Plato and Aristotle only wrote in passing about humor as they discussed other topics, but both recognized that sometimes humor comes from laughing at the misfortunes of others and both warned against the way mockery and laughter can make you lose your self-control. Thomas Hobbes, in his book *Leviathan,* takes it a step further and identifies that the reason we laugh when bad things happen to others sometimes is because we suddenly realize (or feel) that we are much better than the competition. If viewed only as an attack or a way to display arrogance, that makes sense. Some philosophers and psychologists disagree with these ideas, and they don't resonate perfectly across time and cultures, but there's no doubt that we laugh at some jokes precisely because it makes us feel like we're better than the butt of the joke.

Comics depend on this humor when they impersonate politicians or celebrities. The punch at superiority works in this context when the people being mocked are already powerful—they are already in the public sphere, and it's unlikely a joke at their expense is going to knock them from power.

But this kind of joke or humor won't land well between equals or if the person telling it is punching down at someone with less power or influence. If you're trying to use humor with your spouse that sets you up as better than them, it is going to fall flat and likely result in hurt feelings, especially if the punchline is true.

One thing to ask yourself as you tell jokes or share humor, especially with your spouse, is "Does this joke or statement make me feel like I'm better than the person on the receiving end of it?" If the joke belittles your spouse, it's not funny.

Incongruity

Some humor comes out of the difference between what you expect and what actually happens. Incongruity explains how most comics write jokes today, with the setup (what's expected) and the punchline (the surprise or difference). Some writers discuss incongruity as a kind of absurdity. This is what made Kaminski's joke funny—the difference between his lighthearted poke that it "wasn't a good idea" and the reality of the crashing, frigid surf, which was brutal. Watch for places where something feels absurd or ironic and lean in.

More Humor: You Go First

The first place to look for building humor is inside: stop taking yourself so seriously. When Kaminski sat in the surf with twelve guys cursing him on either side, he chose to point at himself and let himself be the butt of the joke. It worked. Note that he wasn't denigrating himself or tearing himself down. He made a joke that owned his part in the torture while admitting it wasn't great—an understatement under the conditions. That's what made us laugh. If you can find ways to laugh at yourself or not take yourself seriously, you'll make everyone around you more at ease.

One time in a business meeting with our staff, Jason was pacing (as he often is), and he got more animated with each pass. Finally, Erica fussed at him.

"Do you have to pace like that? It's distracting," she said in a playful tone.

In that moment, Jay could have had his feelings hurt, he could have been embarrassed, but instead he leaned in.

Jay's face broke into a grin. "I could stop, but I'm like a shark. I have to keep moving or I'll die, you know, it's part of my swagger."

We both started laughing and others on the team joined in. It was such a memorable moment that we built some social media content around it later. Jason made the choice to lighten a moment by laughing at himself and inviting others in on the joke.

Find ways to lighten the mood by looking at your own behavior first. Instead of letting yourself reach for sarcasm or hurt, can you laugh something off? Can you turn it into something more lighthearted?

If Jay had reacted with anger or hurt to Erica's comment, she would have apologized in front of the team. That's just who we are and how we've learned to operate over time. If you're hurt, don't try to pretend you're not. Hidden resentment builds up over time and will explode sooner or later. But if it's something small that you won't replay in your head for days, find a way to laugh at yourself.

You'll also want to be honest about your own history with humor. We're not asking you to change what makes you laugh—that might not even be possible. But if you come from a family that uses harsh, biting sarcasm to laugh at each other, often resulting in hurt feelings, you need to make sure that any negative patterns you experienced don't work their way into your marriage. Use the questions below to help.

What Makes You Laugh?

When was the last time you had a deep belly laugh? A movie? A meme online? A cat video? A joke your five-year-old told you? If you can't remember, start paying attention to what makes you laugh and smile. What loosens that tension in your chest, even if it is just for a moment?

What Makes Your Spouse Laugh?

Initiate a conversation with your spouse about what makes them laugh, but also think about when you last heard them laugh. What do you notice that makes them smile? Can you detect a pattern?

Some might argue you can't plan for humor to happen, but you can prioritize fun together and be aware of what makes your partner laugh. If you've ever watched a short video online and sent it to a spouse or friend, you know the power a quick share like that can have.

Shared Fun

The other way to invite more humor and lightheartedness into your marriage is to have fun together. There are a number of studies that show the couples who play together create more positive emotions about each other, leading to stronger bonds. Those stronger bonds make a huge difference when you face something catastrophic. But you have to invest in that time now—before the crisis hits.

Play can balance out the monotony and stress of daily life. Think back to when you were dating. Did you do the same things every time you got together? Probably not. You likely tried new places or activities, made new memories, and took yourself less seriously. Try to revisit some of that feeling by planning something new to try.

When we say play, we don't necessarily mean games or competitive sports (for some couples those are battlegrounds that do everything BUT offer positive feelings toward each other). Play involves downtime that can be unstructured, just hanging out, hiking, or exploring something new without a specific objective in mind. It can be trying new things together or just daydreaming. Find ways to spend time together that help you enjoy each other's company and embrace fun. A new activity is also a great way to practice not taking yourself too seriously, and it may give you opportunities to develop inside jokes. Whatever you choose to do, find ways to have fun together. We have always played games together, especially card games like hearts, spades, and rummy. Early in our marriage Jay was way too competitive, which led to some arguments and hurt feelings, but over time, he's learned to take it less seriously and we've had more fun, together and with friends.

When Humor Goes Wrong

Humor sometimes won't work, and not just because you don't land the joke. Here are a few comedic impulses that definitely won't strengthen your marriage.

No Picking

We've all been around that couple who pick on each other. It starts with gentle ribbing, maybe even good-natured at first. It can be verbal or even physical—a light tap on the arm or leg, a gentle shove. But make no mistake, if you are picking on each other to be funny, sooner or later it will go too far. Picking on each other in front of other people is the most damaging, since the others present may not understand your dynamic. One or both of you might feel embarrassed to be treated that way in public. Others may misinterpret your playful ribbing as disrespect, which might lead to problems, especially when you're around family or people you work with.

If you can manage to both dish and receive it without inflicting damage, then make sure you are communicating that clearly and be aware of how your picking lands. If something goes too far, apologize sooner rather than later, note it, and refuse to use that kind of humor again knowing it hurts your spouse.

No Sarcasm

Sarcasm pointed at other things can be funny, but when you use sarcasm directed at your spouse, it will harm your relationship over time. Sarcasm expresses contempt—every time. If you come from a family that regularly uses sarcasm, this can be a difficult habit to break. You may be using sarcasm as a defense mechanism to protect yourself in those situations, or to go on the offensive, zinging someone else with your words before they can hurt you.

But remember that you and your spouse are on the same team. If you weaken them, you weaken yourself. Don't do it.

If you're trying to figure out if your sarcasm is hurting your relationship, ask yourself, "Is this making my partner feel closer to me or further away from me?" If your sarcasm is pushing them away, it's not going to help you build an invincible marriage.

Fun Lab: Find What Works

Can you get better at fun and humor? Yes. And it doesn't need to feel like drudgery—it should be, spoiler alert, fun! But it will require some intention and mindfulness as you work on it.

Watch a show or video clip that one of you finds funny or humorous. Then switch. Take a minute to talk about what made you laugh the most. Pay attention if one of you doesn't get the humor. It may mean that kind of humor won't work to defuse a situation. If it's a joke that your partner finds derogatory or insulting, guess what? You don't get to call them sensitive or tell them to toughen up because it's "just a joke." You need to care enough about your partnership that if your spouse gets hurt, you feel that pain and will do what you can to avoid causing it.

If you try some humor and it falls flat or goes too far, own it and apologize. Then do better. Give each other a little room to try things out, and be quick to forgive. When you're learning something new, nothing shuts it down faster than judgment and criticism. Find ways to encourage each other and you may find yourselves laughing and becoming more connected in no time.

INVINCIBLE MARRIAGE MOMENT

Humor and fun are tools that not only help you enjoy life daily, but are lifelines during tough times. Stop taking yourself so seriously and take time to laugh and play together.

REFLECT

1. What makes you laugh?
2. How well are you turning to humor in your marriage?

3. How are you cultivating fun and lighthearted moments together?

FIRST STEP

Find a way to play or have fun together this week, even if it's uncomfortable at first.

CHAPTER 11

Support in Failure

After completing his degree as a part of the Navy's Seaman to Admiral program in 2004, Jason joined a new SEAL team and began the year of workups in preparation for deployment. In July 2005, Jay landed in Bagram, Afghanistan, a dangerous area of operations where SEALs had already been lost in combat. It was obvious from the start that there were some conflicts inside the team, but Jay was confident he would be able to perform his duties.

The year had been an adjustment at home, too, with Jay gone as much as he was home, but we stayed connected. Even when he landed in Bagram, Erica was able to get weekly phone calls with him via satellite phone unless he was out for an extended mission. We were finding a rhythm.

But nothing could have prepared Erica for the email that came one day in September 2005 after a combat mission went wrong, and Jason had made a bad call. He'd acted with the information he had, believing he was acting on behalf of his other brothers in the battle, but he'd also defied an order. And no one seemed to have his back. He couldn't tell Erica the details of the mission, but he said a mission had gone sideways, everyone was okay, and he was waiting for disciplinary review.

As Erica read the email, both anger and sadness flared in her chest. She knew Jason's position in the SEAL teams was everything to him—he'd fought to get back into action after finishing his degree program, and now because of a situation and environment that had imploded on him, his dream was on the line. Our livelihood was on the line. And she was still back in Virginia with three young kids trying to make our household work with him gone. More than anything she was grateful he was out of harm's way for now, but she worried that disciplinary action would crush Jason.

In the moment, she knew he needed one thing, and she delivered when he was able to call her and relate what details he could: "Jay, we'll get through this together. I'm here behind you. No questions."

Jason grappled with the part he'd played, recognizing that he needed to better lead himself if he expected to be able to come back from the humiliation of the incident in that Afghanistan valley. It was a dark time as Jay waited to hear his fate in the SEAL teams from the higher-ups. He finally got word that a disciplinary letter had been written, outlining his errors in judgment, but he would be given a chance to redeem himself and have the letter shredded. But the punishment that stung most was his assignment to Army Ranger School upon their return to the States. Jason knew he would be targeted as a SEAL, and he would spend two miserable months in Georgia and Florida with no contact with Erica and the kids to learn stuff he felt he already knew. When he made it through Ranger School, he knew he'd be thrown right back into the eighteen-month workup schedules that accompanied another six-to-eight-month deployment. The impending time away from his young family wore on him—it was a two-year sentence, and he would have to fight every step of the way to restore any semblance of respect with the SEALs.

Jason was home for six weeks over the holidays, but he spent most of it brooding, replaying the events from Afghanistan. Even when the leadership of his new team said that he had a clean slate to build on, Jason still nursed his anger, knowing that no matter how clean the slate, everyone, everyone was just waiting and watching to see when he'd screw up again.

Everyone except Erica. She was unwavering in her confidence that he'd get back to the teams he loved.

Ranger School began in February 2006, and Jason began with a terrible attitude, still resentful that he even had to be there, hating every moment he was treated like a new recruit instead of the combat veteran SEAL he was. On the third day in the field, they were sent out to a land navigation course, one that Jason was sure he could do in his sleep. Hell, he'd taught land navigation. But he hadn't done it using the same tools the Rangers required them to use, and Jason ended up failing the course. Instead of humbling himself, he gave in to the frustration, had a verbal altercation with the Ranger instructors, and quit. That's how low he was. The never-say-quit Jason Redman exploded and told them he quit, heading back to the barracks.

He called Erica. "I'm coming home," he said.

Erica couldn't contain her excitement. "When?"

As Jason began to explain that he was quitting Ranger School and getting out of the Navy, that his career was done, Erica went quiet.

"Are you still there?" he asked.

"I'm here," she said.

"What do you think?" he asked.

"I can't wait to see you. If this is what you want, okay. We'll figure it out," Erica said, no judgment, no criticism.

We hung up and Jason headed back to begin packing. Erica looked around our home calculating what she needed to do before he got home. Unsure what it would all mean, but confident we would work through it.

Imagine her surprise when the next day, Jason called back.

"So, I had a meeting," he started. A senior leader whom he deeply respected had made a call and challenged him not to quit, not to throw away his career and all he'd dreamed of in the heat of the moment. And Jason finally felt like he knew what he needed to do to rebuild himself and lead again.

"I'm going back into Ranger School, so I won't be home like we hoped."

He could hear her tears on the other end of the line, and he bit the bullet to deliver the hardest part. "I am not allowed to finish with my class. They are rolling me back thirty days to a new class, and I'll be here until the next class starts. I can't come home."

Erica was overwhelmed, and her frustrations spilled out over the line. It wasn't easy juggling the house and three small kids. She missed him. She knew that the rollback meant even more days when she wouldn't even be able to hear his voice. Once her tears and anger were spent, though, she exhaled. "I know this is what you need to do. I'm mad right now, but I'm still behind you. Go finish and come home."

But even that resolve was tested in ways Erica could not have predicted.

Failure Is Inevitable

Given enough time, everyone experiences some kind of failure, whether a health diagnosis, a business failure, a character failure, a family crisis, or anything else that upends your life. It would be nice to believe that we can avoid failure, but we can't.

How do we deal with catastrophic failure? And how do we support each other through failure?

You may feel you have a good handle on what you would do if you were ambushed, but it can be incredibly painful to watch someone you love face this kind of failure. So much feels out of your control, and the fallout may threaten your own well-being.

For Erica, she had to watch as Jason struggled with the near-collapse of his career, partly caused by himself. In the midst of this, she had a choice about how to respond. She could respond out of anger, blame, or even shame, or she could be a source of positivity, trust, and optimism, supporting him as best she could in the midst of the crisis. She chose the latter.

How do you want your spouse to respond when you've lost your job? When you've gotten a challenging health diagnosis, or when you're caught in the cross fire of an ugly family dispute? Would you rather have your spouse support you or join in with others in kicking you while you're already down? Of course, we want to be loved unconditionally and supported fully, but that's not as easily done in practice.

Failure can be devastating. When your spouse loses their job, how do you feel when you have to take on extra shifts to make ends meet? When you lose your insurance coverage? When things feel like you'll never recover?

Why do so many spouses have trouble supporting their partner when they experience this kind of setback?

The biggest three reasons we've seen are fear, pride, and judgment.

Fear is usually the first response when things go wrong. But it's what you do with that fear that will make a difference in your marriage. If it's a professional failure, as Jason's was, and your salary and benefits are on the line, that's scary, especially if you have kids. Fear might cause you to lash out, attacking your partner for being the source of your stress, or even to shut down by emotionally distancing yourself from your family, especially your partner. In that heightened emotional state, you might even find out how easy it is to say harsh things that attack the person, not the problem. It's okay to feel afraid of the future, but you must seize control of the fear and know that even when your spouse makes huge mistakes, you can work through them together.

Pride is the second reason partners don't support each other well in failure. When Jason sat thinking about his decision to quit at Ranger School, all the stories of his family serving ran through his mind. He thought about his kids and how he would have to tell the story of how and why he left the Navy, and how painful that would be over and over. He didn't want to be known as a quitter. Erica knew he wasn't a quitter, that he was working through things on his own, and she trusted that whatever happened, he would come to terms with his decision. But she could have reached just as easily for shame, her own pride wounded by his predicament. After all, we were part of a SEAL community outside work too. She knew the wives of other team members. She could have been embarrassed and reacted from a place of self-preservation. She didn't. She was able to separate him as a man from his actions and mistakes, and because of that, she could continue to stand beside him. If you find that you are in a place where you are embarrassed and ashamed of your partner's actions, make sure you reach for empathy. Don't you think they are feeling the same thing? They don't need more shame heaped on their head. They need your compassion. Even if you disagree with their actions, even if you hate the way they handled themselves, you can choose to see the best version of them even when they are caught in the middle of the worst version of themselves. Think about how powerful that is, and how you might be the only one who can remind them of who they are down deep.

Finally, judgment keeps us from supporting each other well. It would have been easy for Erica to say, "Jay, you're a freaking Navy SEAL, you've done far more than Ranger School can throw at you, just do what they tell you each day and get through it." On one hand she would be right, but on another, there's a thread of judgment there that can tear down your partner.

Most of us like to help. We're problem-solvers by nature, so when our spouse comes to us with a huge failure, our natural response is to go to work solving it. If your partner asks for help, that might indeed be the right action, but more often than not, they just need us to listen and support. If we immediately jump in with solutions, those can easily sound like criticism.

No matter how clear a solution seems to you, let your partner figure things out unless they ask specifically to talk through solutions. And even then, make sure the way you share ideas doesn't veer into judgment or criticism. Feedback gently asks questions and works to build up rather than tear down.

Leave the decisions to them and let them know you'll support them whatever they choose. In the midst of Jason's near-career-ending failure, Erica chose to support him, to be a force of positivity in his life and not another place of criticism. It would have been easy to kick him when he was down. It would have been easy to give in to the uncertainty of the situation and berate him. She didn't.

Failure is inevitable. Remember that when your spouse is going through a difficult season. Next time, it will be you, and you'll need their support.

Be a Safe Harbor

Failure, like conflict, will expose any cracks in your relationship. When something goes south, who do you call first? If it isn't your spouse then it reveals a lack of trust. Is it that you don't trust your partner because of how they've reacted in the past? Or is it because you try to isolate and solve things yourself? Either one is a problem for a marriage that wants to be invincible.

Your shared mission, training, and regular communication affect how well you turn to your spouse when things are tough. If you lose your mind every time your spouse shares something that's gone wrong, don't expect them to feel safe telling you when they've lost their job. If you instinctually hide your highs or lows from your partner, figure out why that is and fix it. Sometimes your own history keeps you from being honest; maybe your parents didn't react well to such news. Or perhaps your partner didn't react well the last time you hit a rough patch. If that's the case, you need to confront that pattern head-on. It's a conversation that can begin as simply as, "I'd like to tell you about something hard that happened, and I'd just like for you to listen. Sometimes it feels like you want to fix things or like you get upset about my problem and that doesn't help. But I love you and I need your support." Your partner may feel defensive the first time, probably the first ten times. But pretty soon, you get better at letting people own their problems and learning to trust them to try. Jay was able to be honest and clear with Erica about the problems in Afghanistan and at Ranger School because we'd used those years while he'd been at school building trust and a foundation that could stand the storm.

That's what a safe harbor does—it creates a place where you can retreat when things outside are unmanageable and overwhelming. Let your marriage be a place where you both know that every time something happens, you can come home and it won't be made worse. Be a place where your response to failure is, "Damn, that's hard. I love you and I know that you're going to figure it out. What can I do to help?" There may not be anything you can do to help directly, but your unfailing support at home? That's everything when your spouse is fighting battles outside your home.

You can't make your spouse a safe harbor, but you can work on becoming one yourself. Start by remembering that you are part of a team that wants to remain committed to each other. That sounds repetitive and basic, but it is the first step to being a person your spouse trusts with everything. Then make sure that you aren't trying to control things that are out of your area of responsibility. When your spouse shares things that have gone wrong, practice responding with compassion instead of fear or judgment. Learn how to take a deep breath, to not let fear, pride, or judgment win, and instead reach for compassion. That's how you build a safe harbor. Now, it is both of you together against the storm outside.

Check Expectations

Unrealistic expectations can keep you from being able to support your spouse when things go wrong. What were you expecting to happen that didn't? Erica expected Jason to do his deployment and come home with his unit. That didn't happen. She expected him to go to Ranger School and come back two months later, stronger than ever. It didn't quite happen that way. Sometimes you are holding unrealistic expectations and don't even realize it—both expectations for yourself and for your partner. If you expect to never fail, you're in for a terrible reality check. If you expect yourself or your partner to always be happy or never to change, you're being unrealistic. Just holding those unrealistic expectations will feel like failure when they aren't met, so pay attention to what expectations you have and check to see if they are helping you become stronger as a couple.

This is part of why the divorce rate is so high in special operations, law enforcement, and first responder marriages—expectations can be so mismatched from reality that spouses can't handle it. You think it's going to be cool to be married to a Navy SEAL or Army Ranger until you see the insane training schedule and end up spending most holidays alone. You think you've got a plan for the future, and then your spouse is catastrophically wounded, and that vision goes out the window. And it's not just in our world: too many people are marrying a fairy-tale version of a life that cannot possibly live up to your expectations.

Some expectations are nonnegotiable: fidelity to each other, mutual respect, shared responsibility, and whatever else you've communicated in your values. But a lot of other stuff is negotiable, and you need to be willing to let go of getting everything you want to embrace what your partner can give in a tough situation. If you struggle with perfectionism, you're going to find your spouse's failure in direct conflict with your own desires, and that's going to lead to judgment and criticism. If you expect to have an ideal relationship that never has problems, you're going to be disappointed.

The answer is to become more flexible. Let go of unrealistic expectations and embrace reality, even when that reality is painful and hard. If your spouse loses their job, you're going to have to change your budget plans until something else comes along. Don't make it worse by ranting for weeks about the vacation you're having to cancel, the expenses you're having to cut, the luxuries you can no longer afford. Your marriage is more valuable than all those things put together. It's your expectations that have to change, and you can choose to do it without resentment. Are you going to be sad? Angry? Of course. There's nothing wrong with that. Erica responded to Jason's call from Ranger School with tears and anger—those were natural responses to the news Jason wasn't coming home. It wasn't anger directed at him, but at the situation. But when you nurse those feelings instead of your love and support for your partner, the expectations undermine your recovery.

Know Your Role

If your spouse has a hard day or a catastrophic season at work, remember that it isn't your job to beat them up further. Erica instinctively understood this as Jason went through his struggles in Afghanistan and the resulting stint at Ranger School. He was already beating himself up, feeling like he'd blown everything. She knew that her words could either build him back up or tear him down further. She chose to build him up. It wasn't her job to critique his job performance—nor to go in and tear down the people in his command who hadn't supported Jason. Her job, as she saw it, was to support Jason and to let him know that no matter what happened, we would get through it together.

Depending on the failure, it's normal to feel helpless at first. That's a gut reaction. But don't stay there. When Jay made a questionable call in Afghanistan, he let the helplessness of the situation overshadow everything else. Nothing seemed like it would help. His attempts to justify or explain what had happened to teammates fell flat. He felt utterly alone in an organization that requires you to have a swim buddy at all times. He realized much later that he had needed to find a way to take responsibility and lead himself better. That realization came with time and the effort that Ranger School required. Imagine if Erica had refused to support him when he came home or refused to listen when he had to roll back to the next Ranger class. He might not have made the remarkable recovery he did, and our marriage would not be what it is today. Her role was to let him struggle while letting him know she was beside him every step of the way.

Is that easy? Hell no. But your role when your spouse faces failure is to put aside your own feelings for a minute and find ways to build up your spouse authentically. Erica couldn't come to Ranger School and cheer from the sidelines. She could let him know she was handling things at home and that she'd be there when he finished, proud of all he'd accomplished.

While Jason worked through the waiting period and second class of Ranger School, Erica was managing a storm of problems on the home front. Her car broke down. Appliances quit working. One of our kids had raging ear infections that necessitated surgery. She handled it all alone because that's what the season required. Did it suck? Yes. We wouldn't wish a season like that on anyone. But she knew her role was to take on a little more at home for a time, so Jay could work through the ramifications of returning to his Navy career. His return was a victory for both of us. It took both of us to get through that time, and whenever Jay talks about that time period, he always credits Erica's support for getting him through it. Don't think that just because your role is a supporting one that it isn't absolutely vital to the mission's success. It is.

Affirmation

When you're in the middle of failure, your self-esteem takes a hit. Suddenly every negative thought you've ever had about yourself becomes a playlist that blares on a loop in your brain and maybe even out loud in self-defeating talk. When your spouse is in that space, be intentional about affirming their best qualities—and the best qualities you share as a couple. Be aware of the positive and negative impact of your words. Don't make stuff up—that's disingenuous and almost worse because it suggests there's nothing good to say. Instead, think about what drew you to your partner. Think about the good times you've had together. Remind them of their strength and what you admire about them.

Affirmation from a spouse who knows you inside and out can be the most life-giving motivation a person can experience. Your spouse may be the only person who affirms you and your identity during a tough time. Jason had very few people in his world reminding him of his potential in Afghanistan and later in Ranger School. He was grateful for the handful who did encourage him to dig deep and remember what was important to him, but most often it was Erica and her steady voice, her unwavering support that kept him going.

When Jay suffered catastrophic injuries on the battlefield and fought for his life, Erica came into the hospital while his head was half bandaged, tubes running everywhere, and kissed him— assuring him of her love and partnership. Together, we drew from the knowledge that we'd made it through difficult periods in our marriage before this one. It gave us strength. We knew how to make mistakes and correct them because we'd done it so many times before.

Our brains gravitate toward the negative, but you *can* refuse to see only the bad. Instead, find ways to see the good in each other. Thank your spouse when they listen, when they help, when they begin to make hard choices that are the right ones in the situation. Let them know you're in this together and you love them. Find little ways to inject more kindness or attention in your marriage, whether it's texting little jokes or funny videos, fixing or buying a favorite dessert, or just spending an extra hour on the couch or in bed. Remind each other that the problem is not bigger than your relationship.

What If the Failure Is Inside the Marriage?

The most challenging obstacle a marriage can face is a breach of trust, whether through infidelity, lies and deception, or some other violation that devastates the bond between you.

We don't like the word "quit," but there are times in life when it makes sense to fall back, reevaluate, and make a plan that's best for you and the people you care about. If you do the same things over and over again and expect things to change, that sounds like a miserable life. So, what do you do when the failure is inside your marriage? When one or both of you has broken your vows and promise to be partners?

We haven't faced this obstacle in our marriage, but we've walked alongside dozens of couples who have been in the middle of this type of ambush. Some of them made it out, building a stronger marriage, and others parted ways. We've seen both be the right choice. So, what do you do in the face of an affair, lies, or other breach of trust?

Here's what we've noticed in our community.

Assess the Situation with Honesty

Get brutally honest about what has happened. Was it a one-time lapse of judgment? Or is it a pattern of behavior? What is the degree of severity? Do you feel it's something you could forgive and move past if your partner is truly sorry and takes action to correct it? You have to be honest with yourself and your partner. There's no sense telling them you'll forgive them for gambling away your nest egg, and then bringing it up every time you look at the budget. Even some one-time lapses may be severe enough that they can't be recovered from.

Seek Help to Get Support and Clarity

You're likely going to need help. Whether it's a counselor, a trusted pastor or chaplain, or some other professional, you need someone with an objective view to help you ask the questions you need to ask before you make decisions. If your spouse's failure stems from addiction or mental health disorders, you need to know the ramifications of that condition before you make any decisions. If the failure stems from long-held communication dysfunction in your marriage, you may need a couples therapist to teach you new skills to relate to each other differently. Arm yourself with information.

Own Your Stuff

Sometimes betrayal goes both ways. Own the part of the problem that belongs to you, not to minimize your partner's actions, but to free you to see the context where the failure has happened. If you're the partner who chose an affair, you don't get to blame your spouse. You made choices. Own them.

Make a Plan and a Choice

Once you've assessed the situation with help and owned your part of the problem, you can decide on a plan forward. Sometimes we see couples choose to divorce when the trust is impossible to restore or one partner refuses to change. Sometimes couples overcome incredible odds, taking baby steps together toward restoring that trust one action, one day at a time. It won't be a perfect path back—you're going to make mistakes and have to adjust as you go—but if you choose to be each other's most important teammate, then you approach every aspect of your life and relationship differently. Execute the plan and keep choosing each other.

Have Patience

The final piece of the plan is extreme patience. Broken trust is incredibly hard to overcome. It takes time and consistent positive behavior over time to rebuild that trust and your broken credibility. When Jason failed as a leader in Afghanistan, making that bad call on the battlefield, he broke the trust of his teammates, with many of them asking for Jason to be kicked out of the SEAL teams. Thankfully, he had leaders who believed in him and gave him a second chance. That did not mean his teammates felt the same way. They did not trust Jason to make good decisions on their behalf and they made Jason well aware of that. He knew it would take time to prove he had truly changed, that he could make good leadership and tactical decisions. If there has been a breach of trust in your marriage, don't expect it to be fixed overnight. It may take months or even years to fully repair that breach. But if you truly believe in your relationship then continue showing your partner you have changed and are fully committed to be the partner they deserve.

One last thing on breaches of trust. Now seems like a good time to say again: violence or abuse is never okay. If you're in a situation where you or your kids are being hurt, it's time to go. That's one breach of trust that is utterly unacceptable. Don't give one more chance, one more day, one more time. It might be your last. Seek out the resources you need to safely exit, and reassess once you're safe.

Aside from abuse, the question becomes one of your mutual willingness to start making changes toward being better teammates for each other. For us, we were well-matched from the outset, and while we've always had disagreements, we have never let them overshadow our absolute commitment to each other. Our struggles required us to learn new skills and to practice our commitment in the ways we prioritized each other and our marriage.

Was it easy? No. Worth it? Absolutely. Just because something is hard or the progress is slow doesn't mean it's time to quit. If you're committed to each other, your values align enough, and you're both working to look out for each other? Stick with it. You might be surprised what you can do together.

Every Failure Is an Opportunity

If there's one thing we've had to learn over and over in our marriage, it's that every failure is an opportunity. We don't seek out failure, but when it comes, we try to recognize what the failure is, our role in it, and we begin to take action together as quickly as possible to address it. Above all, we turn to each other. We've practiced it so often that it feels unnatural not to turn to each other first. If you're still building trust, keep taking the risk of being vulnerable in failure knowing it is an opportunity to grow together. There's no better training ground than failure, so when it comes, embrace the lessons it offers and use it to strengthen your marriage. You'll be unstoppable.

INVINCIBLE MARRIAGE MOMENT

When your partner encounters failure, you can support them when you check expectations, know your role, and affirm who they are. Your marriage can be not only an asset in the midst of loss, but a safe harbor that shelters you through the storm.

REFLECT

1. What failures have you already experienced in your marriage? How did each of you respond? How have you grown from it?

2. What do you need from your spouse when you're facing a crisis or failure outside of marriage?

FIRST STEP

Which one is hardest for you in the moment: being a safe harbor, checking expectations, knowing your role, or giving consistent affirmation? Discuss with your spouse and listen to how you'd each like to be supported.

CONCLUSION

Your Marriage Is an Asset, Not an Obstacle

If you take nothing else away from this book, remember this: **your spouse is your most important teammate.** Treat them as such and you'll find a satisfaction and connection you only dreamed might be possible. An invincible marriage is made resilient through shared respect, friendship, and a common mission. If you've just gotten married, and you're wide-eyed, in love, and giddy, maybe those first difficult pangs of conflict or irritation send doubt coursing through you. All of us have looked at our marriages and said, "Wow, this isn't how I thought it would be. It's harder than I expected."

But in an invincible marriage, you finish that statement differently: "Wow, this isn't how I thought it would be. It's harder. *And better.*"

If you're still in those early stages of marriage, trying to figure it out, our hope is that this book has given you the tools to set aside the fairy tale and replace it with something far better. The foundation you will build in these early years can carry you through adversity, conflict, and even crisis. We know firsthand. We were young, dumb kids in love once, too, making mistakes and making amends, over and over.

Because that's the key: believe the best about your partner and marriage and you will approach any problem you face *together*. See your marriage as an asset and treat it like one.

If you're early in your relationship, vow to be careful with your words, knowing trust is extremely hard to win back once broken. Establish and use Rules of Engagement when fighting so you don't "shoot each other" and do permanent damage. There's a lot that can be repaired when you screw up or make mistakes, but some things and words are hard or impossible to undo.

Building a strong foundation means choosing friendship and clear communication over selfishness and pride. Build rituals and a unified front through your shared time and embrace of humor. Don't let the little things pile up, thinking you can overlook problems to keep the peace. Fight fair and with an eye toward keeping your marriage strong. It's hard to harm your spouse if you view them as the most important teammate you have.

You don't need money to do this either. We had very little starting out. We went places together, played games together, hung out together. We went to parks and bars and over to see friends. The point is we did it together and enjoyed our time. We still look forward to seeing each other, to planning adventures, even if they're just down the street. We don't love all the same things, but we've got enough common interests and respect for everything else to know we're pursuing a marriage that lasts.

It's not always easy. You might have to work to try a lot of things one or both of you hate to get to that place. Isn't it worth it though? If nothing else, you're creating memories of things you tried, and those memories might make you laugh for the next fifty years. And that is the goal: to be together and happy for at least fifty years!

Too many young couples pursue each other wildly while dating and then get married, only to return to a life that they lived before being a couple. It's not going to make you a stronger person or team.

If you're a couple who has been together for longer and lost your way, you've hopefully started to rebuild the friendship that brought you together in the first place. Maybe you've read all the way through, knowing your marriage isn't really an asset like you want it to be. What are the red flags that you already notice? How can you start addressing those one at a time?

Your marriage might be more obstacle than asset if you:

- Live two separate lives, not really connecting often.
- Spend more time at work or with friends than with your spouse.
- Don't spend time together aside from household logistics.
- Have lost interest in sex with your spouse.
- Feel stuck, routine, just going through the motions.
- Constantly fight or never fight.
- Your spouse isn't the first person you want to tell good or bad news.
- You aren't making plans for this week, month, year, decade together.

Whatever the obstacle, you can conquer it together. You have to be on the same side though. It starts with accountability, owning your part in the relationship, and we don't care how one-sided it seems, both of you have played a part in getting to where you are today.

When you commit to treat your marriage like an asset again, go back and reevaluate your values. Do you truly align on those life-shaping beliefs? In the areas where you don't align, can you compromise out of respect and trust?

Then, get out your calendars and your banking accounts. What have your priorities been? How can you realign one area this week? Make time for a date and talk about anything but kids, work, or logistics. Remember the person you fell in love with at the beginning. Then keep at it, realigning your priorities until you find you're more in tune with each other and the life you were hoping to build together. And celebrate along the way—it isn't going to be perfect. You're going to screw up. Okay, so screw up. But get back in there to apologize and try again.

You don't have to leave on some crazy cross-country adventure to inject your lives with more fun and spontaneity. You just have to be a little creative and a lot willing to try. Do things that scare you and trust each other. You can't build trust if you know how everything's going to turn out.

SEALs aren't born trusting each other. They learn strategies and skills to become highly effective teammates. You may not always agree with your teammates, hell, sometimes you don't even like them, but you love each other and would fight to the death to save them. They would do the same for you. This is an invincible marriage: two people willing to press into life as a team with each other's backs—no matter what.

Your spouse is the most important teammate you will ever have. Start living like it.

BONUS SECTION

The Invincible Marriage with Kids

As parents, we have raised three kids to adulthood, and each of them is thriving in their own unique way. We weren't perfect, but we've found that the principles and the Overcome Mindset that guided Jay's career back on track and kept our marriage invincible have benefited our children as well. This bonus chapter includes what we've learned about being a couple raising successful kids.

In early 2004, we attended Jason's grandmother's funeral with our two children. We had long before decided two kids was the ideal number for our family. But at the funeral, Jason saw his dad with his three kids, and it sparked something in him.

"I think I want another kid," he told Erica one evening after the funeral.

Erica exhaled. "Really? We've always said we just wanted two."

"I think I've changed my mind."

Erica felt reluctant but agreed to consider it. She thought about all she was juggling already with his impending training workups and deployment schedule. Another baby would be a huge adjustment. But maybe we had time. After all, it had taken us almost a year to get pregnant with our first baby together. What was the harm in starting to try?

A month later, Erica brought Jason a positive pregnancy test. His jaw dropped.

"Are you kidding me?" he said.

Erica balked. "What? This was your idea. You had better get happy quick."

Jason laughed and hugged her. "I don't understand how it happened that fast."

Erica gave him a knowing smile. "I think you do."

Even when your marriage is in a good place, even when you're in agreement about having kids, actually bringing one home introduces new challenges, no matter how ready you think you are. That can be made more difficult if one or both of you weren't sure about having kids in the first place. Hopefully, you spent time during dating talking through those values around family, and if your stance changed, you've communicated that. If not, it's time to immediately revisit it because if one of you is checked out or resistant to having kids, then a pregnancy and birth is going to be full of resentment and negativity. Do not spend one minute believing that your spouse will change their mind once a baby comes—you cannot build a life around a gamble like that when there's another little human involved. It isn't fair to any of you.

The one thing we know about life with kids? It's unpredictable. It isn't going to be a fairy tale, Christmas-card-worthy experience day in and day out. One of our kids had a heart defect that required constant observation and specialized medical appointments. Two of them had severe acid reflux that caused them to projectile vomit constantly. You're up at all hours, exhausted, worried you're going to screw them up, but still doing your best in a sleep-deprived fog. Doesn't that sound romantic?

It isn't. Not for us, and not for you.

Kids, while awesome, take a toll on your marriage. The majority of couples, 67 percent according to a study by the Gottman Institute, report feeling less satisfied in their marriages for the first three years of parenthood. So the first thing to realize is that you aren't alone if you are feeling displaced or disoriented after you have kids. It's going to take some time to figure it out. That knowledge, that it will be tough for a bit, can help you both make it through the transition.

That said, you absolutely can prioritize your marriage, and it's imperative you do so if you want your marriage to remain healthy and even grow. You also need to stick together because parenting requires an iron-clad partnership. Kids have their own personalities and desires, and you have far less control than you think. They will try to divide and conquer you, even at a very young age. It's a crucible for marriage, and it can absolutely make you stronger if you approach it as a fully committed team.

Think about the goals you have as a couple with kids. If you're like us, you want two things: you want your marriage to kick ass and get stronger each year and you want your kids to emerge from childhood as well-adjusted, contributing adults. And we've done it. You can too.

As we think about the beliefs, habits, and decision-making process that we have used raising our kids while we kept our marriage strong, it comes down to that mindset we've talked about through this entire book: you are a team. Equal partners with equal say and equal responsibility. Is that how your marriage is working now? Because if it isn't, it's time to rethink how you're approaching it and make the needed changes to become invincible.

Action

Here are the areas where we most often had opportunities to level up our partnership while parenting: duties, discipline, and decisions.

See where you need to get better aligned to be a stronger partner and team.

Duties

In the Protector community especially, it's easy for the serving partner to abdicate responsibility for "kid stuff" to the other spouse. We get it. Jason's schedule was extremely unpredictable for years, which made it hard at times to share childcare and household duties as much as we'd like. But when he was home, he was all in. He changed diapers. He shared in the sleepless nights. He looked around and saw things that needed to be done with the house or kids or whatever and did them. When we had to make tough decisions about a health procedure or school, we made them together. Was it perfect? No. But over and over again, we knew that we were a team, and our kids were our shared responsibility. Both parents need to be involved in all aspects of parenting.

Two things might be at play as you think about how you're currently sharing (or not!) duties and time raising your kids, especially if only one of you is primarily managing the kids.

For some spouses, cultural or family expectations have dictated that you, too often the mom, are responsible for all things kid related. Maybe you even want that responsibility, but don't let it become your whole life. We've seen many couples who are disconnected because managing the kids and their activities has sucked every bit of time and energy from them. It's easy to understand how this happens: That first year is intense. A baby has so many needs, and whoever is closest most of the time will fill those needs. It doesn't take long before one or both of you gives up trying to share those duties because it feels easier in the moment.

Sometimes when a spouse tries to take on more responsibility or duties around taking care of the kids, their partner is critical or controlling, insisting that something can only be done one way.

If the way your spouse is trying to help is causing danger to your child, okay, correct them, but otherwise? Let them figure it out unless they ask.

You can't hover over a new parent and expect them to feel competent, especially if there's a running commentary about how they could do this or that better. Stand back and let them work it out. We guarantee the person you loved enough to marry and make your teammate is smart enough and committed enough to adjust and grow the same as you. But they will never do it if you're constantly interfering.

If you're the parent who tends to be around less for whatever reason, like Jason was, don't check out and think your spouse doesn't need you. They might actually be able to manage everything with you gone, as any military spouse can tell you, but that isn't the goal. When you're home, engage fully, not waiting to be told what to do like another child in the home. You're an adult. Notice what's happening around you and jump in fully—both as a parent and as a spouse. Also, let each other vent and listen. While Jay was often gone, Erica was intentional about not lacing every phone call with a laundry list of what was going wrong, but sometimes, she just needed her biggest supporter, the man she loved, to know how hard things were, even when there was nothing he could do.

We've seen time after time how couples center their whole existence around their kids, forgetting to prioritize their marriage. Then what happens? The kids graduate and leave home, and the two of you look across the room at each other and feel like strangers. You've been roommates who love and care for the same kids. Don't let that happen to you.

Keeping your marriage strong while you parent your rugrats isn't going to be easy—there will be days you wonder what you've gotten yourself into. Days you want to quit. But you aren't going to do that. Don't quit on your kids and don't quit on your spouse. Parenting difficulties are an opportunity to work through something as a team that will make you stronger. The reason SEAL teams are so strong is because they've had to depend on each other through unthinkable conditions and scenarios that may have put one or all of them in mortal danger. The higher the stakes, the greater the opportunity to come out stronger. Parenting those kids is a similar challenge some days. Lean in and do it.

Discipline

Discipline is an area where you can discuss your values and priorities ahead of time, but nothing will test those ideas until you are actually staring down a defiant two-year-old tornado.* Here's where you have to take into account both your own partnership as parents as well as the individual personalities of your children. We aren't parenting experts or anything, just a couple who has traveled this road together with three kids.

The first thing you need to take into account as you work together on a discipline plan for your kids is the natural bent of your children. Some kids only need a stern look while others need to face more serious consequences.

You're going to have to unpack how each of you were disciplined as a child. What you think worked on you may not be the right choice for your own children. Talk about it together as a couple, staying open to each other's experiences and ideas. If you have an area of disagreement, do some research, or get an expert on the line to help you figure out the best way to move forward. If one parent is super overbearing, scared to do anything wrong or to let your kids fail and the other is determined to give them space to figure things out, you are going to have

---

* Ours ran on plutonium and crack—I swear it's true.

conflict. Go back to your goal: healthy, functioning kids who be-come healthy, contributing adults. You can't do everything for your kids or make all their decisions for them. Sometimes you have to let them fail, as long as they aren't involved in anything genuinely dangerous. As an instructor in SEAL training for pla-toons, Jason regularly evaluated a team's progress during train-ing missions. Even when the platoon was making mistakes and poor decisions, as long as it wasn't life threatening, instructors wouldn't step in. The failure was an opportunity to learn. That's hard as a parent, but you know they will grow from the failure or pain.

One area to really watch as you discipline is thinking about how you talk, first to each other and then even how you speak to your kids. If you're dismissive, yelling, spiteful, or critical in every interaction with each other as parents and then with your kids, you aren't going to get the results you want. We've all been out in public where we've heard adults talk to each other or their kids in cringeworthy ways. Don't let yourself go there. If you were filmed talking to your spouse or kids, how would you feel watching it back? Don't get defensive, get proactive. If you were always yelled at as a kid, you're going to have to make a conscious choice not to do the same when you feel like you need to get through to your spouse or kids.

Instead, think about how your words and actions are being received.

When Jason was a kid, he found himself in a period where he was grounded over and over until the days became intermina-ble. It felt like he would never get out. It sapped his motivation. We have to think about how our discipline is being received. If it causes our kids to check out, we need to find ways to give them a light at the end of the tunnel and opportunities to atone for mistakes.

As a result of those experiences, it was important to us to give our kids opportunities to earn privileges back, to practice working their way out of failure and restoring responsibility as well as they could. We might feel like grounding one of them for six months after they are caught sneaking out for the third time in a row, but six months is an eternity for a teen, and it probably won't inspire the behavior you actually want to see. Start smaller and give them attainable opportunities to prove they can do the right thing. This is what we did when one of our kids found themselves in some trouble. We didn't want to crush her. We wanted her to see that while her actions had consequences, she could correct those actions and begin to earn back her privileges through demonstrated responsibility over time.

Your kids are going to make mistakes. They are going to do dumb stuff. Didn't you do dumb, irresponsible things as a kid? Yeah, your kids will too. Discipline is an opportunity to pass on your values and to practice what to do when you make mistakes. For us, our kids knew Redmans don't quit. We sometimes screw up and have to make amends, but no matter what, we don't quit—especially on each other. Discipline will really challenge those beliefs and values and force you to live them out in front of your kids.

Decisions

Parenthood can bring on decision fatigue faster than almost anything else, and many decisions feel like they have long-term consequences. That's why it's so important to get on the same page not only about the decisions you make on behalf of your kids, but the process you use to get there. From deciding on childcare options to school choices and activities, decisions need to be approached as a team. Work from your values instead of defaulting to what your parents did, what your friends are doing, or God forbid, what someone online tells you to do. It's tempting to live your dreams through your child or to feel like they have to compete with everyone else when they don't. Remember that you're working to help your child become a productive adult.

We really got to practice this art of compromise in parenting when our oldest son was finishing kindergarten. Erica had attended Catholic schools growing up. Jason had attended public schools. Both of us had a positive experience. When Austin went to school, we knew the schools in our area were known as being good overall, and that's where he did kindergarten. But he was delayed in his speech and needed a little more support. He was one of the youngest ones in his class. When we reached the end of the year, the school said that while he hadn't passed the skills needed to move on, they would move him on to first grade if we wanted them to.

We were both against it. We didn't want him to be behind and frustrated his entire school career, so we began researching other options. We didn't make a lot of money, so there was that to consider too. No school was going to be perfect in every single way, so it was a matter of finding the right fit for the right time period for the child in question. Erica took the time to research all the available schools to do the full due diligence before we decided. We sat down together and narrowed down the list, and then we went together to visit the schools left on our list, keeping our son's unique needs in mind.

At the end of it, we found the right school because by Christmas that next year he was excelling.

We compromised to do what was best for our child and his specific needs. Those needs changed as the years progressed, but we still wanted our process to remain unified as we made decisions for our kids. You can too.

The Power of Example

It might take time to adjust and make sure you're approaching parenting as a team, but it is absolutely worth it. Not just for you, but for your kids and grandkids. Everything you do as a parent? Your kids are watching. If you are health conscious and work out, they will likely follow you. If you speak respectfully and lovingly to each other like team members who want the best for each other, your kids are going to pick that up. If you sit on the couch and watch television as your spouse runs around doing all the carpooling, childcare, and housework, there's a good chance that your kids will grow up and perpetuate that cycle. If you are a goal setter and an entrepreneur, your kids are more likely to be that way too. Set the goal now to show your kids what a good relationship looks like.

You want to watch your kids thrive now and in the years and generations to come? Invest in your marriage and your team mindset now. Make corrections if you need to. Be humble and if your kids are old enough, talk to them about the changes you're trying to make to be better for each other and for them. Model what it looks like to transform your life and you give them more than a powerful example—you give them a roadmap to their own invincible life.

Business Partner Marriages

We knew from the outset that we wanted to include a section of the book that applied the Invincible Marriage principles that have helped us run successful business ventures together for decades. We've run multiple companies, including a nonprofit, a speaking bureau, coaching, consulting, and so much more. This section is for those of you who have the unique concerns of a business partner marriage.

N ot all spouses can or should work together. But for us, being business partners has brought us closer and made us into the powerhouse team that we are today. But it definitely comes with its challenges too. Many of the principles we've discussed so far—from communication to conflict—can be applied to the business world, but the stakes are doubly high when those interactions affect both your income and your most significant relationship.

One such challenge came to light one day when we were driving to Richmond, Virginia, for a speaking engagement. The week before, we'd had a call with a new employee, and she and Jason had spun out a ton of new ideas. Some of the ideas were viable, but she was abrasive and in essence attacked many of the systems we already had in place. It had been an overwhelming call, especially for Erica, who understood on a granular level how much of the day-to-day operation would be disrupted based on the call.

On the drive to Richmond, Erica hoped to address a few of her concerns while we were already on a work trip. What better time to discuss than when you have a few hours together in the car with someone's undivided attention? That was the first miscalculation.

"I had some questions about the call yesterday," Erica said.

"Yeah, it was good. What'd you think?" Jason asked.

Erica took a deep breath. "I don't know that we can manage all that at once."

"She had it all lined out. We can definitely do it." Jason looked over at Erica briefly and then focused back on the road.

"No, I know she had a list, but I don't think you realize how much work that's going to be, and most of it will be on me. You're traveling and I'll be the one initiating all these changes. We're moving in too many directions and it's overwhelming." Erica tried to keep her voice even.

"We've gotta make changes though if we want to grow," Jason argued.

The conversation went round and round, neither of us really making headway.

By the time we arrived at the venue, both of us had steam rolling out of our ears. Jason stormed into the building to get ready to speak and Erica took a minute to collect herself.

When she went inside, the event organizer could immediately tell something was up.

"Is everything okay? I haven't seen you all like this before," he said, concern etched on his face.

"Just a tense conversation on the ride up. He'll be good," Erica said, hoping she was right.

When you work together, you don't get to disagree with a colleague and then come home and vent to your spouse the same way you might in a traditional job. The lack of separation between home life and the business creates friction and a lack of balance at times. But you can and must still be able to discuss those work problems. But when your business partner sleeps in your bed, you have to handle those conversations a little differently.

Erica needed to vent about that call. It had been overwhelming and her feelings were valid. She hadn't realized it would be such a heated conversation or she probably would have saved it for the next day. In hindsight, both of us realized that we needed to ask for a time-out and promise to revisit it after the trip when we were both able to focus on the problem instead of arriving at a speaking engagement irritated and grumpy with each other.

We've run several businesses together now, and we're proud of what we've built. We've learned a lot about how to work together on the business side to make sure we stay solvent and protect our marriage at the same time. Here are some things to consider if you are already or planning to be in business with your spouse.

Make a Plan

Obviously, any business requires a plan. If you don't have a plan, you don't have a business. You have a recipe for failure. Don't wing it, especially if you're bringing your marriage into it. You need clear goals, and ways to measure your progress.

In the beginning, that might be difficult, since you may need a little time to figure out the metrics that will tell you whether or not you're being successful, but at least have a target you can adjust as needed with clear timelines established as checkpoints.

At the bare minimum, you need to know who your company is, what you're offering (products or services), who it's for (market analysis), how you're going to reach those people (marketing strategy), and what it costs to deliver, along with the financials and budget with a full accounting of the time and expense it's going to cost to deliver your product or service. Not sure about one or more of those elements? Get help before you sink any more time or money into your venture.

Don't be like children running a lemonade stand who think they've made a killing with $10 after a couple hours selling, when they forget to account for the lemonade mix their parents bought, the water, pitcher, table, signage, cups, and the time they spent setting everything up and on the street selling. Do the research to make your business viable and strong.

Cash flow is KING. One of the reasons we have run and grown six successful businesses is we are relentless in cash flow management. Know where money is coming from and going and project out the next three months so you can plan for the ups and downs of business. It means turning liabilities into assets, diversifying your income streams, and looking for recurring revenue models. If you don't know what we mean here, it's time to do some intensive business research before you go any further.

You owe it to each other to write the best plan you can. Once you have done your due diligence and have a clear plan, you can begin to think about how to run your business together.

Clear Roles

To make a business partnership work, whether it's with your spouse or someone else, you have to know and use each other's strengths and weaknesses to your business advantage. Each of you is unique and brings different skills, perspectives, and ideas to the table. Spend some time identifying those strengths before you

go any further, and it will save you a ton of heartache (and probably money) later.

The first thing to establish is that your business is an equal
partnership. Just like in marriage where both people get equal say
and decision-making power, in business, you can't expect both
partners to be empowered to act if one of you is constantly under-
mining or minimizing the other's decisions. We have never felt
like Erica is running or working for Jay's business. It has always
been our business. How are you talking about your business right
now? Is it focused more on one of you? Or on you as a couple?

If you haven't been in a full partnership before (or even if you
have), it's essential to make sure you define who is going to take the
lead on which parts of the business. This doesn't mean you value
one role over the other. It's more like recognizing that nothing
works well without all these parts moving together in harmony.
Defining those roles can help keep you from getting sidetracked
when you hire or have outside contractors wondering who to report to. If you know your main roles and areas of responsibility,
then it's easy to identify who needs to check what on the regular.

It took us a while to figure out our roles and to lean into what
each of us did best, and the resources with the Entrepreneur Operating System (EOS) helped tremendously. EOS is a system that has
helped us structure our business, from clarifying our mission and
roles to the nitty-gritty reports and review process to ensure we're
always moving toward our business goals. Jason is a visionary—
he thinks in big ideas and wants to be driving forward on every
front. He's more the face of our business, traveling, speaking, and
all the outward-focused fronts we run.

For Erica, she's the integrator—the person who manages all the
small details that bring the vision to life in day-to-day operations.
She's creative and organized, well-suited to being the glue that
keeps us together.

Those roles overlap at times, with Erica contributing to vision and Jason working on details, but overall, we know where each of us excels and contributes most effectively. But you can see how if Jason starts spinning out more ideas than we can realistically execute, Erica is going to pump the brakes. She can immediately see all the individual steps and the workload that will land on her desk if we scale too quickly or branch out in too many directions at once. When Jay notices Erica is overwhelmed juggling all the responsibilities she has in the business, Jay is quick to ask if she needs a listening ear or if we need to hire someone to manage part of the load.

Just identifying your strengths and being able to communicate how you best operate within those strengths will move your business forward in new ways. You'll spend less time arguing about the day-to-day operations when both of you know specifically which tasks and outcomes are for you to execute. Your employees will know who to ask when they have a question or when something goes wrong because you have clear areas of responsibilities. It's just like parenting—critical to be united—because employees will play Mom against Pop just like the kids if you don't have clear roles and a unified front.

Also, of course there are parts of business that neither of you enjoys. Figure out how you'll get those undesirable tasks done, whether shared, rotated, or outsourced. The clearer you are about who is doing what and when, the better.

It's likely that one of you has a better head for the business side while the other might be stronger on ideas or creativity. Know your own strengths and weaknesses and lean on each other. For us, we both have an entrepreneurial spirit and the work ethic to match. Be honest about whether or not you and your spouse are both 100 percent committed to the work it's going to take to run a business together. So many couples are unbalanced, and it creates drag. You can't move as quickly or effectively if one of you isn't on the same page, whether related to the vision, goals, or execution.

In addition to tapping into our strengths, we've also thought about how we can each help the other shine and thrive in the business. It's back to that team mindset. If you're thinking about how you can help your spouse be their best at the same time you both build the business? It's a winning combination.

Once you have your area of responsibility, own it and take initiative to do it well. In SEAL teams, we're expected to know our expertise and deliver it without waffling or disclaimers. If your partnership has been unbalanced, where one of you has constantly felt unsure about your contribution, it is going to take a mental and physical shift to change that dynamic. If you're unsure about what to do in the role you've taken on, do the research and present ideas together until you come to a consensus. If you do the research and you know the right direction, don't ask permission. Communicate what the research has shown and why this direction will work best. Affirm each other as you try things out, returning to your business goals and metrics to measure your progress.

When something goes wrong in your area of responsibility (and it most certainly will), communicate what's happened and what contributed, own the problem, and begin looking for the best solutions. There's no room for the blame game in business when your marriage is also invested. If you made a mistake or miscalculation, don't hide it or try to minimize it. Own it and ask for help if needed. You built this business. You can rebuild it, even if you need to make some changes to do it well. Running a business is an exercise in resilience, and you can't fall apart the first (or hundredth) time something goes wrong.

Work Boundaries

If you're both passionate and committed to the business, you will need strong boundaries to keep work from spilling over into every other part of your lives. We have definitely fallen into this trap a few times over the years, but we usually right the ship pretty quickly when one or both of us realizes we're on the burnout train or we're missing connection outside of work. It's one of the best parts about working together, because we know each other and our business inside and out, including when one of us needs to take a break for the health of the individual, marriage, or business.

Sometimes a boundary is as simple as going out for a work-free-zone dinner, or establishing times you can check work-related email or calls. Be flexible, but make sure you still prioritize your couple and family time too.

Adapt and Overcome

If there's one thing we've learned in business the last ten-plus years, it's that things change. If you expect to set something in motion and never touch it again, you're going to find it failing or dead in a matter of time.

Change can come from internal shifts, like when your own desires or passions change, or it can come from the outside where the market or some other factor out of your control changes.

When those shifts happen, you have to ride that wave together. Here's where the trust you have built as a couple goes a long way to insulate your business from storms and change. We recognize that everything we've built could be gone—our home, our business, our assets—but if we have each other, we will figure out the rest together. We're going to do our best to keep our business strong, but the reality is that our marriage is worth more than a million-dollar business, a home, or anything else we might build.

When you come to a friction point as you run the business, don't try to gloss over it quickly. What is causing the friction? Can you explain the parts of the problem you disagree on? Just being able to pull back as a couple and see the business problem as separate from you as a person or couple can help you face it with more clarity.

One of the hardest parts of building something is that it feels like your child, and you don't want to change or admit when it isn't working anymore.

More than that, your business will be stronger when you trust each other to try things out. If Jason is super passionate about developing one part of the business in a certain way, and Erica isn't sure about it, she listens, asks questions, and then trusts that if the idea fits within our business model, goals, and budget, Jay can run with it. We've thrown a lot of ideas on the wall that didn't work, but those ideas helped us develop debriefing skills to identify when things don't work. Part of the fun of entrepreneurship is that thrill of unknowing. You have to be able to embrace risk, trusting that if everything goes wrong, you can fix it together without bitterness or resentment.

Even when things are going great on the business end, you may find that you're both exhausted and stretched thin. When that happens, pay attention and reevaluate how you're doing as a team. Do you need to pull back on something to keep your work in bounds? Or hire someone to take over a part of the business to free you up for the most important work? These conversations need to be happening weekly, so you're in touch with what's happening and how the work is impacting each of you. Don't wait until a problem has run one or both of you into the ground and bankrupted you to address it. Be watchful and honest about what's happening, trusting each other.

In addition to those weekly check-ins, you need regular annual and seasonal reviews. We tend to charge hard on things for a year or two and then step back and realize we've got too many irons in the fire. We feel the press of being overextended and want to simplify. This is why your business plan is critical. You need to be looking at your daily operations and monthly profit/loss statements against that initial vision. What's working? What isn't? Does something need to change?

Even more important is the need to reevaluate what your business is. What are we and what are we doing? Are we still moving in the direction we want to be? What are our priorities?

We always look at the metrics. For example, we ran a coaching group for several years and loved the interaction with clients, seeing the ways they were overcoming incredible odds using the tools we provided. But when we began to look at the metrics, how much time we were spending versus how much profit it produced, we found a disparity. It was costing us 40 percent of our time, but the profit margin was significantly lower. We tried restructuring it, dropped and added services, but ultimately, as a business, it didn't make financial sense. We chose to shut it down—a gut-wrenching decision when we knew it was making a difference in our clients' lives. If something isn't pulling the weight it needs to be, but we think it still has value, we make a plan, giving it a certain amount of resources for a certain period of time to see if it starts delivering. If it doesn't, then we have to let it go. We can't be attached to a thing that's losing money and just keep throwing more time and money at it. We can admit that it was a path we needed to try, that we learned from it. And now it's time to let it go for the health of the overall business.

In Business and Marriage

Running a business with your partner is a double-edged sword, because your hopes and dreams and your mortgage and your vacations are all tied to your business. When profits are down and you're both working to the bone on something that isn't delivering, it can be hard to navigate that space, especially when you're together so often.

Find ways to keep your marriage separate from business, so that when the money shifts, your relationship doesn't. Remember that your marriage is most important—make sure you treat it as such and you'll reap the dividends of your relationship far beyond the life of any business venture.

ACKNOWLEDGMENTS

We would like to extend our deepest gratitude to Joe Bunting and Sue Weems for embarking on yet another project with us. This book has been years in the making, and we are so thankful for your unwavering belief in it and your dedication to helping us bring it to life.

A heartfelt thank you to our agent, Linda Konner. You stepped up when we needed it most, embracing this project with excitement and enthusiasm. At a time when we were starting to question whether we would find a publisher who truly believed in our story, you were steadfast in your communication, support, and commitment.

Lastly, we are deeply grateful to Nick Amphlett and the entire HarperCollins Publishing team for believing in this project and our story. Thank you for your support in helping us tell our story and for making a positive impact on others' relationships.